Purposeful Parenting
The Early Years

JACI MUN-GAVIN

Copyright © 2012 Jaci Mun-Gavin

All rights reserved.

ISBN-10: 1477561889
ISBN-13: 978-1477561881

Cover Design by Tonya Seiler

Unless otherwise stated, scripture references are taken from
The Holy Bible, New International Version ®
Copyright © 1973, 1978, 1984 by International Bible Society.
Used by permission of Zondervan Publishing House.
All rights reserved.

DEDICATION

My handsome husband – it is a privilege to parent with you. Life is so much better with you in it. You're still the one.

CONTENTS

	Acknowledgments	i
	Introduction	1
PART I: THE PURPOSE OF PARENTING		
1	Outcome Based Parenting	6
2	Purpose Beyond Product	9
3	It Takes Three	21
PART II: GENERAL PARENTING		
4	Respect For All	28
5	Loving on Purpose	52
6	Practical Pointers	60
7	Discipline	68
8	Developing Godly Character	85
9	Teaching our Children About an Invisible God	94
PART III: SPECIFIC PARENTING		
10	Rock-a-bye World	104
11	Bringing Up Warriors	122
12	What a Girl Needs	131
13	Family Planning	138
14	On a Personal Note	149

ACKNOWLEDGMENTS

Thank you to my precious children, who were so encouraging throughout writing this book, always asking me how it was going.

Thank you to my husband, who happily served me and our family, who believed in what I was doing and cheered me on, and for being my 'go-to' guy for parenting advice and Godly wisdom.

To Tonya Seiler, thank you for designing this fantastic book cover and for convincing me you're my biggest fan.

To Deborah Mun-Gavin, thank you for your editorial expertise, both as a psychologist and as a mom.

To Catherine Smith, thank you for your sharp editing eye and for your love for me and my family.

To my parents and parents-in-law, thank you for the innumerable lessons you have taught Richard and I – so much of how we parent is because of your examples.

I am so grateful to my Father in heaven for providing us with a purpose for our lives, and for His word that is so rich with instruction, promise, and hope.

To all my friends and family, thank you for being so kind as to help me believe that I had something to say. I hope this book will live up to your generously high expectations!

INTRODUCTION

My husband and I were the first in our circle of friends to have a baby. I am a relatively carefree person, adapting to change quite happily, and was quite blasé about my new duties as a mom. I loved my baby dearly, but my 'mother's heart' was, as yet, quite underdeveloped.

We continued to do everything that we had done before the baby arrived, which is why we found ourselves one Sunday evening at a restaurant with a huge crowd of friends, newborn baby asleep in the pram behind my chair. We had all come straight from a church service and had spread out to a few tables around the restaurant. At our table, the girls were sitting on one end, deep in conversation, and the boys on the other end were playing practical jokes on one of the other tables. Unbeknown to us girls, they had just sent our food bill over to the other table.

Suddenly, my girlfriend opposite me exclaimed, "Where's your pram?" I spun around, only to find my pram, and our newborn baby, had both disappeared. Writing this now, many years later, I still choke up at the memory of that moment.

But for me, luckily it was just a moment. I looked across the restaurant and through the glass window at the table outside, and saw that those dear, playful friends of ours were watching us with grins on their faces, my precious pram, covered in a pink blanket with my babies name embroidered on it, was parked right beside them.

I smiled through the window at them and opened my mouth to say, "Good one - you had us all for a moment there," but instead, all that came out was a choke of emotion, and I burst into tears.

The boys rushed inside with our pram, and apologised profusely, insisting that they had overstepped the boundary and regretted their joke. My husband and I reassured them that we totally understood the heart of the prank, and were 'so' not offended... But neither could we stop the tears from flowing at the emotion of the whole thing.

And do you know, I cried for three days! I went to sleep that night sobbing, and when I woke up, fresh tears welled up in my eyes. I wasn't, at any moment, upset about the prank itself, but for the first time I realised, on a deep level, that my baby was completely vulnerable, and I had allowed her to be taken without even noticing for several minutes. Not only did she not know my telephone number but she didn't even know my name! My eyes were opened to the weight of the responsibility that had fallen heavily on my shoulders, that I had not yet consciously grasped.

I realised that the pain I had had in my sternum for the few weeks following her birth, was not just due to the strain of labour, but was rather the dread of responsibility manifest in my body. Since then, I have experienced the same pain in my chest while cradling and nursing each of my newborn babe's that followed.

What a fearful and wonderful thing to be responsible for another precious life!

So now that we have this joy, and we want to 'do it right', how do we do that? This book is comprised of my ramblings as I have discovered some of the how, and some of the why, of parenting, as far as I can tell.

As I have shared my thoughts with friends and beyond, it has seemed that my learnings and discoveries have helped more than just me, so I have compiled them, to see if, in God's wisdom and grace, He will use them to help others. It is a very personal and real journey I have gone on as a mommy to my particular children, so I hope you find it relevant and are able to apply some things in your home, too.

It is relevant to note that some of what I have written are Godly principles, based on the bible, and some are applications, which are my husband's and my interpretation of these principles. You certainly don't have to do things the way we have done them if you already have a better way.

PART I

THE PURPOSE OF PARENTING

1 OUTCOME BASED PARENTING

To start off with I want to explain how we came up with some of the 'how' of parenting. My husband, Richard, and I were trying to make a decision about how we wanted to educate our children. Were we going to use preschools? Were we going to school them at home for preschool, or maybe even for longer? Did we believe in boarding school, and should we have our one-year-old's name down for high school already?

I never realised before that our choices would be so varied and so difficult. I thought the pattern was kind-of laid out for us: you send your kids to the preschool and primary school with the best reputation in your area, and then make a plan, even if it means bonding your house, to send them to the same private high school that your parents sacrificed to send you to.

When I realised that there were actually many more options available to us than that, it made me start to really question what I thought was best. My wise husband focused our decision making by pointing out that we really needed to determine what kind of children we wanted to produce by the time they were eighteen or so, so that we could decide on the best methods and resources to help us to achieve that... And thus we coined the phrase 'Outcome Based

Parenting' or OBP for short. The phrase was a bit of a family joke, because at the time the school education system had fairly recently launched the OBE system, or 'Outcomes Based Education', and it was coming under quite a lot of criticism.

We gave some careful thought to our 'product' (please don't hold me too strongly to calling my children 'products' - you understand we were just trying to parent intentionally, with an end goal in mind). We thought about them entering the world as adults, and what we would hope to have imparted to them for them to 'succeed' in their lives... Again, we would have to first define 'success'! What would we want their confidence levels to be? What skills would we want to give them the privilege of acquiring, both for life, work, and pleasure? What character would we want to develop in them? It was important to think about what their purpose in life would be and what they needed to be able to achieve this as adults.

These questions had a radical impact on the decisions we made for our children and family, both immediately, and in the years to come, as we had a picture of the 'end-goal product' of our parenting.

The bible speaks about children being arrows in their fathers' quiver. Psalm 127: 3-5 says, "Behold, children are a heritage from the Lord, the fruit of the womb a reward. Like arrows in the hand of a warrior are the children of one's youth. Blessed is the man who fills his quiver with them!"

We looked at our parenting as shaping and sharpening our arrows for a particular flight, a particular target, and a particular purpose.

An interesting result of having such purpose and intentions for our parenting is that it gave me an intense sense of urgency. I have so much to teach these little people and so many things I want to impart to them! It kills me to waste their time because the days of their childhood are flying by and I have no idea how I'm going to fit in all the biblical teachings and incredible stories, all the world education, all the skills development and all the character development that I have in mind!

It is incredibly helpful and motivating to have an end goal in mind. However, knowing what we want to accomplish with our parenting, although important, is not enough. We need to know why would we want to produce kids in the first place. Is there more to parenting than just the outcome? Is there more reasoning behind our methods than just the end results? Are there other goals and motivations along the way?

2 PURPOSE BEYOND PRODUCT

The bible says about a good mother, in Proverbs 31:28, "Her children arise and call her blessed; her husband also, and he praises her."

I love that verse. Her children call her blessed. That word has a double meaning, which is so essential in capturing successful motherhood. The joy is a two-way necessity. The mother is blessed. She is privileged to have children and she knows that she is blessed. She is blessed by them. But she is also blessed by them, in that they praise her. As they live in the knowledge that she loves and appreciates being their mother, so they are filled with joy and praise her for the mother that she is.

Now I know I'm still in the early throws of motherhood – my eldest child has only just entered preparatory school (Grade 4) – but it appears to me as I observe many mothers at different stages around me, that motherhood is jolly hard work. It starts off with a bang as you spend your first few months hanging over a toilet, and it just doesn't seem to get any easier from there. Right into a child's adulthood, I have prayed with mother's still weeping and losing sleep over mothering their children. As the children get older it seems the demand for skillful, intentional mothering only increases. So I ask myself, why do we do it?

Why would we encourage 'free' woman to become mothers? What is there to motivate us to carry on being a mom when the going gets tough? You start off feeling nauseas and exhausted from pregnancy hormones, then your baby arrives and you spend the next few years nauseas and exhausted from lack of sleep. And then, when your teenager is sleeping through the night and two thirds of the day, and you should finally be catching up on some rest, instead you spend the next twenty years nauseas and exhausted from anxiety over what they're getting up to, and what life choices they're making that are, in your opinion, really way too big for them. Goodness me, but is this all worth it? What's the point?

It occurred to me recently, as I was lying in my bed, in the early throws of pregnancy, feeling nauseas and dizzy, and my children were calling for me, that when the going gets tough in a race, you need a good reason to keep going! I had a friend - she was a good mom, a good wife - and she had prayed for a few years before falling pregnant the first time, and again the second time. She had a tough run of it with her young boys – they were sickly, and the one in particular was in and out of hospital a few times. After a few years of motherhood, she bailed. She opted out. She just left home and went back to living a single life, where she could go to movies when she wanted to, get out of bed when she wanted to get out of bed. You might be horrified at that, but to me, I am not that shocked or surprised that a young mother can get to that point.

Motherhood is an extremely high calling, a calling to sacrifice and endurance like nothing I have ever known before. The Comrade's Marathon, a 90km endurance running marathon in South Africa, is a tough race, but it's only one day. We tick that kind of one-day, painful endurance test off our list the very first day of motherhood – that was labour and birth. The Tour de France is twenty-one days – so the first twenty-one days of having a newborn baby is pretty intense, and for those of us who had normal babies that cry all night, it certainly took us to the edge of ourselves. But it didn't stop there.

We still weren't at the end of the race. Only just beginning! So again, I ask, when the pressure is more than you can bare, and it just doesn't seem to be letting up for the foreseeable future, how do you keep going? Why are we doing this? Why have children?

Before you think I hate being a mom, I don't at all. I love it. It is one of the most fun, wonderful, exciting, rewarding things on earth. A bit later we will look at that as one of the many reasons to have children. But it's when it comes to crunch time, when the pressure is on, that we need to know why we are doing something. We need a reason sometimes, something concrete to hang on to, when you're wondering if you've bitten off more than you can chew.

For His Glory

We have been created by God, in His image, to glorify Him. He is the Creator – He had to create. And we are His workmanship, and we must be what we have been made to be in order to reach fulfillment, and to achieve our purpose. The bible says, "For we are God's workmanship, created in Christ Jesus to do good works, which God prepared in advance for us to do." (Ephesians 2:10)

Let's have a look at God's purpose for our lives and for humankind in general. We need to go back to before the fall of Adam & Eve, before sin entered the world. So let's start in Genesis with God creating mankind, and look at the purpose for that:

Genesis 1:27-28 "So God created man in His own image, in the image of God He created him; male and female He created them. God blessed them and said to them, 'Be fruitful and increase in number; fill the earth and subdue it. Rule over the fish of the sea and the birds of the air and over every living creature that moves on the ground.' "

Not surprisingly, these verses hold two of the major keys for continuing to reproduce and have children. I say 'not surprisingly', because our God is kind enough and sensible enough to let us know what He expects of us and why. It makes sense that He would explain it at the beginning. Before the fall, I'd say it is all the reasons for our existence and the continued existence of mankind. Now that Jesus has come, there is also a third reason to have children, but we'll get to that one in a little bit.

So firstly, in verse 27, it says that God created us in His image. The way He has worded this is so relevant. "God created man in His own image, in the image of God He created him." That man is not mankind, it was man – a person, a being, who was Adam, a full representation of God – a man with a woman incorporated into who he was – Eve had not yet been taken out and separated from him. But God knows that this picture will help people for the next few hundred generations to understand what He is like. So God creates man as one, and then He separates that one into two parts – and He says that this confusing picture is made in His image. A complete being that is two people that can relate to one another and show kindness to one another and prefer each other - this is the image of the invisible God.

And when we take that picture a step further and the two people come together and produce a child, made out of their togetherness, and this child is an image of them, and they love this child, it is a picture of God as the creator and Father of the man. The picture continues.

And in this child, we, as parents, see something of the perfection and glory of God. In addition to that, when an outsider beholds a parent with their child, it is a reflection of God and His relationship with the people that have been made by Him, to be like Him. It's all a bit poetic and it's not a concrete picture – just like a child doesn't look exactly like its mother or father. It's hard to express it in words, which would satisfy our left-brained tendencies, but just like a picture or a poem is not meant to, or able to, be fully concrete, neither is this image that God can show us only through us observing family life.

While I was writing this chapter, we had the privilege of going away as a family to a little fishing cottage in a nature reserve in the mountains. One afternoon, my husband took our children fishing in a little rowboat on the dam. I was sitting up on the lawn of the cottage looking down into the valley and onto the dam. On the hill across the valley to my right was a herd of zebra and blesbok. As I sat there, I asked God to teach me something.

A little wagtail bird landed beside me just then and went hopping across the lawn. I was reminded how God's creation helps us to know Him. I thought, "That one of God's creations tells me something about Him. He's artistic, He has an incredible eye for detail, He loves beauty." As I thought of the way all the little systems in the bird are working together, I noticed, too, that He is definitely super intelligent!

The bird is one of His 'creations'. If God was an artist, the bird would be one of His paintings. If God was a musician, the bird would be one of His songs. Looking around me I saw a number of His pieces of art – there were trees, and clouds, and wind and sun, there were zebra and buck and wildebeest grazing on the hill opposite me. Each was a piece of artwork, representing something of the Artist. Someone who makes a zebra, clearly enjoys surprising people with thinking out of the box. He's got a sense of humour. The heat of the sun and the power of a thunderstorm tell me He's powerful enough to work with any medium. He is greater than those. To quote from Mark 4:41, "Even the wind and the waves obey Him!"

And yet all of these creations are just artworks. They are not self-portraits. An artist's work tells us much about him – but what if we could meet the son of the artist – a child made in his image? Surely that would be the best representation of him. As I was sitting on the lawn, thinking these things, I heard carried by the wind, the voice of one of my children from down on the dam, "Dad?" and his deeper voice answering them in words I couldn't make out. Then the next child, "Dad?" and again the deep and gentle rumble of his response blew up to me with the wind. As I looked at them sitting there - he was rowing all of them, and they were just basking in his presence - I thought, "Now that picture of God I can see!" That is more than

> A parent with his child is created by God to be a self-portrait of Him and us.

just one of His artworks - that is created in His image. I can see God in that scene as if it were a self-portrait. I can see how He loves His children, and how He protects them and provides for them. That is almost as good as seeing God himself. That shows me a lot more about God than the zebra does - God bless the zebra and his humourous coat!

And so, that brings me to my first reason why you and I should have children. It brings God glory. As people look at you loving your children, it shows them something about God that is beyond words or explanation. It takes a picture.

This also puts an onus on us to be good representations of God! Back to the scene of the fishing dam, as I looked at the herd of zebra and buck, I thought, "These animals' exposure to just a few men would shape how they see mankind. Will their experience teach them to trust men or to fear them?" Similarly, as people are witness to our lives and what they represent, they will form an opinion on what parenting and parents are all about, which will shape what they think about the Father of all. It's quite a weighty responsibility to be the representation of the invisible God! "I urge you to live a life worthy of the calling you have received." (Ephesians 4:1)

At a Mom's and Babies' group we have at our church on a Thursday morning, I looked around at the mom's with their little toddlers and saw so much of how God loves us. One young mom, Sarah, caught her baby's eye in the mirror and broke into a big smile. Carike's eighteen-month-old suddenly got panicked and felt lost and she called out to him, "Mommy's here, boy. You're ok. I haven't left you." Chloe was sitting in the corner with her nearly three-year-old, laughing with him about his dirty feet, bringing her sense of humour down to his level. Gill was just quietly watching her two-year-old, Ella, trying to do something on her own, and smiling over her in pride and enjoyment. Each mom there was glorifying God just by being themselves. They didn't know that God was glorified in my eyes because of them, but it didn't matter. The little bird that I saw carried on glorifying God by doing what it was created to do, whether or not anyone was watching. Just as God is glorified with a storm over the sea that no-one sees, so He is glorified by you in the privacy of your own home.

When you get up in the night to answer a cry, when you stay awake praying for a situation your child is in, when you plan a meal that is balanced and affordable, but with as much generosity as you can manage, when you tenderly fold little shirts and socks, when you check on your child before you go to bed, and make sure the temperature is just right in the room – all these things are done in His image and glorify Him. Even if you're the only one who sees them, stop and think of the things you have done and give thanks that your Father cares for you the way He has put in your heart to care for your children. He longs for you to live within the safety and provision of His 'Father-ship', His dominion.

A Role on Earth

The second verse we read in Genesis speaks about stewarding the earth. I was chatting to my husband about this 'life purpose' topic and he was saying that our mandate is to steward the earth and also to bring up our children to be the next generation able to steward the earth wisely. It's interesting that as we have a reason for the 'why' of parenting, it helps us with the 'how'. If we don't have clearly defined goals then we will be very lucky to achieve anything. If we have children just because we think it will be fun to have a little mini-me running around, then it might go something like this:

"Mom, what's my purpose in life?"

"Well, I made you to be a little mini-me! But now that you mention it, you're not doing so well. You're supposed to like ballet like I do. And your eyes turned out the wrong colour. Come to think of it, your purpose in life has not been achieved with much success at all!"

My husband was telling me that we are supposed to raise our children to be the next 'stewards of the earth'. So I said, "So as long as our kids turn out to be tree-huggers, we did ok?" But he reckons there's more to it than that.

When we give our children the knowledge of how to live in a sustainable way, that is important. We must teach them to be responsible and to care for the planet. We must teach them to respect the world they live in and to wield their power with wisdom. They need to respect animals and plants and have a heart to protect species from going extinct.

But there's more: they also should be interested in discovering exciting ways to make the most of our environment – like discovering the potential of silicone. Did you know that the reason computers can be so small and powerful is because they are made of the same substance as sand? Metal, as you know, is a very good conductor of electricity, and things like plastic and rubber are very poor conductors of electricity. But silicone, which is basically sand, is neither very good, nor very bad. Because of this, a very subtle change can cause it to either conduct or not conduct electronic signals, which is the property that makes it possible to build such tiny circuitry within computers! God knew that when He created the earth. He knew about the medicinal properties of certain flowers and leaves and animals. He knew it all, and He loves our delight when we discover it!

The bible says, "It is the glory of God to conceal a matter; to search out a matter is the glory of kings." (Proverbs 25:2) It's like a big game of Hide 'n Seek, and it delights Him when we take the things that He has given us on this earth and see how best they can be used.

So, we educate our children in the areas of math's and science, and weather, and rocks, and plants, and animals, and everything else. We educate them in humanity and in defending the defenseless. They need to know how to steward the people that are within their influence. We teach them about the ways of God, and Godly order, and good governance. We teach them how to build roads, and buildings, how to heal diseases, how to govern fairly and with wisdom. We teach them the value of a good refuse disposal system, and the merit in knowing how to clean and tidy. All of these skills are necessary for the next generation to steward the earth responsibly.

But also, we educate them in the arts of music and dance and poetry and art, because these things bring glory to Him as we imitate His creativity. We teach them how to manage and arrange their homes in a way that brings peace and a safe haven to those who are in it. We mine whatever gifts God has placed within them, whether it be singing or running or anything else under the sun. As we fulfil the potential and calling within us, God is glorified. Not only that, but these things also bring joy to us as we are fulfilled in expressing the gifts that He has placed within us.

> As we call out the greatness in our children, God is glorified.

So, we glorify God in our parenting and we bring up our children to steward the earth and to glorify God in their lives, as well as in their parenting.

While we're doing this, in God's great design, we find great fulfilment. And that is just because He's good. I don't even know if that counts as one of our purposes of why we have children. It's just a by-product of living life the way God intended. And isn't it a wonderful by-product! The things children say! And the laughter they bring into the house! Their delight at discovering such simple things. They say that humour comes from something unexpected happening. So, if a joke has a predictable punch line, it's not that funny. But if you are surprised by an unexpected punch-line, it makes you laugh. For children, so much of life is unexpected, as they have not experienced it before, so they are just laughing all the time. You will tell them the name of a new vegetable:

"What is that mom?"

"It's an aurbegine." And they burst out laughing.

"I didn't expect a name like that!"

Sometimes I notice in a public place, like at the beach, all the older couples whose children have left home are watching the families with children with fondness on their faces, and all the young adults are watching the children as if looking forward to that season of their lives. It just seems that being in the middle of having a home full of children, is right in the prime of life, and people are either looking forward to it or missing it. Having children in your life is like having permanent entertainment. Your home is never dull. Even folding their sweet little clothes is quite fun! Buying them gifts is fantastically fun. And playing with their gifts is also pretty fun, too!

The amazing thing about having children, is that it teaches you something about God (well, lots about God) that you could never otherwise have known. How can we understand how God can discipline those He loves, until we have had our own child disobey us by running towards unprotected water, or running into the road. You think to yourself, "This is worth disciplining for! They can never do that again!" I put my kids into the car one day, and then went back inside to fetch my bag, and my two-year-old, Rourke, put my keys in the ignition and started pretending to drive. I knew that I needed to teach him never to do that again!

And only when we have children, can we understand God's willingness to take any pain onto himself to protect us from being hurt. There are so many things that having children teaches us about God, and I think this fits into the first purpose, in that it brings Him glory as we understand Him better.

Continuing the Mission

My third reason of why to keep having children in this day and age, despite the evil and dangerous world they will live in, despite the overpopulation of certain countries, is that we are on a mission to bring God's goodness back into this world. We have been saved, we have been taught the way back to God. We need to teach others about the way that God has made available for us to find Him in this fallen world, and we need to teach our children to make sure that the message continues for as long as this world still has to exist. Jesus came and brought with Him the way to heaven, the way to a kingdom that is ruled by God and His goodness. We need to teach that to the world for two reasons:

Firstly, we do it because we have compassion on a hopeless and lost generation. We see people around us confused and lost, unaware of what causes the emptiness they feel; unaware of why their lives are falling apart - people who don't understand God's ways, and the way everything works so much better when it is done according to the rules under which it was created. He is the creator, and He made the manual for how things work best. There are people who are slaves to addictions, addicted to substances, addicted to sexual perversion, addicted to warped relationships that make them feel too powerful, or too needy. We tell them about Jesus, and how they can be set free from the power these things hold over their lives, because we care. We tell them how they can escape the just punishment for their sin, because we have a heart!

And secondly, we tell them about Jesus, because we owe Him our lives. He has set us free, and taught us how to be in relationship with our heavenly Father, the way we were created to be. So if He asks us to tell other people and spread the word of how He is The Way, then we do it because we owe Him everything. And for these same two reasons, we make sure that our children are brought up to be gospel carriers to the world.

Because of the desperate days we live in, and the lack of Godly order in this world, not in spite of them, is why we continue to bring children into the world. The world may be overpopulated, but it's filled with people that have not been taught how to steward the earth wisely, and people that need to hear about the way back to God.

So we have children, because there is blessing in that and it is God's gift to us, but even if we adopt children, either way, we do it with these purposes in mind:
- That God may be glorified, for many to see, and when no-one is watching: by our parenting, by the beautiful picture of a child with a loving, protecting, providing, disciplining, training,

nurturing parent, as well as by the beautiful things we do with our lives in the form of being creative and being ourselves;
- That the earth may continue to be stewarded well, that we would protect it and use it's resources wisely and fully, that we would govern with excellence;
- And that the good news about what Jesus has accomplished on the cross would reach all people.

By now, perhaps, all you parents are thinking, "I don't think I'm going to be able to teach my kid to drive a car, now I'm supposed to teach them to drive the Earth? My kid can't remember to take a message to their teacher, two minutes after I've just told them to, now I'm supposed to equip them to take the message of life to a dying world? This is not an easy job!"

I totally agree, which is the reason for the next chapter: 'It Takes Three'.

3 IT TAKES THREE

I witnessed a father the other day, disciplining his son... well, actually everyone in the vicinity witnessed it. He had all the right ingredients: he was a present father, for starters; he was involved; he was disciplining his son; he was protecting his young daughter from being mistreated by her brother, all of which are so great; but he was totally botching it. He just seemed to have no wisdom, either in what he was saying, or in how he was saying it. The poor boy was left hurt, emasculated, confused and embarrassed.

And then a few days later, I had a chat with a lady, who, to be honest, has none of the right ingredients to mother her brood: she has married a widower and 'inherited' his children, but has not yet had any children herself, and has no earthly clue how to raise these kids. And yet, amazingly, as she told me of one particular situation where she was clueless and at her wits end, I realised that she had displayed the most incredible wisdom in her choice of words to her children, and had turned their hearts toward her and brought healing and understanding to them.

The difference? She had fallen on her knees before speaking to her children, and cried, and begged God to give her wisdom to get through to them, so that she would not fail them or Him. He (the father in the first example), sadly, does not know God.

Christians, there is no way you fully realise the incredible pool of wisdom that we swim in, just by knowing God, and being exposed to His Word, and His people. And add to that, we're allowed to actually go to Him with each individual situation, and ask for specific guidance - it's no wonder our kids are turning out alright!

So next time you're wondering how to answer your pre-adolescent's difficult question, or even trying to figure out why your potty-trained toddler is suddenly refusing to make a 'No. 2' in the toilet, go to the Source of all Wisdom, the perfect Counsellor, and the Creator of bodily functions, and get some REAL advice!

Hebrews 4:16 "Let us then approach God's throne of grace with confidence, so that we may receive mercy and find grace to help us in our time of need."

It's all about Him, and having the confidence to approach Him with our questions. We have been robed in Jesus Christ's robes when we accepted His forgiveness, and we can walk into the throne room of God as royalty who deserve to be there. We don't slink in and beg for crumbs. Rather, we are seated at His table, and chat to Him as easily as a son to his father.

I have, thus far, only given you the why's of parenting, because, as I wrote in the beginning, the why, the purpose, helps us to decide on the how. If we don't know the desired outcome of our parenting, then we're going nowhere, and we can expect our kids to turn out as a product of chance.

But first up, I want to give you one very particular how, that I rely on very heavily.

I will explain it by quoting a blog that I wrote:

Superhuman Wisdom

I'm so grateful God knows everything, and I know Him. Because this parenting thing often takes super-human wisdom!

My darling child was getting herself involved in fights with her friends, and into trouble with her teachers, way too often. And I didn't know how to help her. It breaks a mother's heart when you know your child is being hurt, and yet something she is doing must be bringing it on.

I sat down with her the other night and we prayed together, "Oh God, you know what is going on in her life. You know why she keeps getting into trouble and involved in fights. Please give us a key - something she can change - that will help her to avoid these situations."

And, being a good God, He answered!

He gave me a picture to share with her:

"When we are driving, if we are going a little left, we need to pull right and if we are going a little right, we need to pull left. Now in the bible, there are lots of instructions that seem to be opposite to each other - like for example, the bible tells us to stick up for people and 'defend the defenseless', but, it also tells us we should mind our own business. The bible tells us both these things to help us stay in balance. Now, in life, we are driving, but it's like our eyes are closed and God needs to tell us whether to pull right or pull left in order to stay on the road. Now for you, my girl, you have a very kind heart. You want to help people. When you see someone doing something wrong, you want to tell them. When you see someone doing the wrong thing in class, you want to tell the teacher. When you see your friends arguing, you want to get involved and try to help solve it. But God is telling you, you are pulling too far left. You are being too helpful and too involved. You need to pull a bit right. You need to start minding your own business a bit more."

And then I showed her a verse. 1 Thessalonians 4:11 "Now make it your ambition to lead a quiet life, to mind your own business, and to work with your hands, just as we told you. In this way, your life will win the respect of outsiders, and you will not be dependent on anybody."

Well, when she saw that God had written the answer for her in black and white, she was blown away! She was so excited. How is it that correction from God is always a joy? She was amazed that God had given her three clear instructions, which she knew applied to her situation. As she thinks of something to 'tell on' or 'fix' she must think:

- Be quiet
- Mind my own business
- Keep working!

And in addition to giving clear instructions, He had given her an assurance - this would help her to regain the respect of her teacher and her friends! As they saw her cheerfully working hard, minding her own business and not trying to get involved in every fight and every misgiving, they would start to see that she had changed and want to be around her again.

Added to that, she also told me, "Mom, God has told me another verse that applies to me. He says that before trying to tell my friends what they are doing wrong, I should 'take the plank out of my own eye'. That's true, hey Mom?"

Well, what could I say? God is doing a great job parenting the darling children He has put into my care! And thank goodness for that!

So, this is my 'how' in everything: I ask God for wisdom. Whether it's why my baby is waking up, or how to mould the lives of my pre-adolescents, I rely on Him. And I rely heavily on His word. Just about everything I read helps me with one or other situation.

Coming back to Proverbs 31, verse 26 says, "She speaks with wisdom and faithful instruction is on her tongue." This noble woman who is praised by her children and her husband, is a mom who is soaked on God's word. She knows God's instructions for each circumstance that she is in. She relies on His wisdom, and she is able to instruct her children in the ways of God in their lives. She is a helpful confidant and teacher to them. She reads God's word and commits it to memory for those moments when she might need it on hand.

And how do we ever get there? Verse 27 says, "She watches over the affairs of her household and does not eat the bread of idleness." No-one ever said it was going to be easy! Being a mother, as we've read, is a high calling, and such a noble task, surely requires hard work.

> Your parenting may cause people to see God in a new light!

But remember, in verse 28, "her children arise and call her blessed". She is blessed to have children and she knows it. It is a high calling, yes, and a demanding calling, sure, but to think that your life has such purpose! The lessons you teach today might still be being taught in generations to come. Your lessons, and your menial tasks, may cause people to see God in a new light! It may result in eternal life with God for some, and it may result in new discoveries, in the defenseless being defended, in the land being governed fairly.

Furthermore, it is our privilege to coach and support younger mothers in their new role, to teach these things to children who might not be getting the lessons at home, to include in our families those who are without mentoring and parenting, and to ensure that the generations to come do not forget their purpose.

PART II

GENERAL PARENTING

4 RESPECT FOR ALL

I think a launching point for bringing up children in a manner that brings God glory, is not surprisingly a rule that can be carried through in all of life. The overwhelming atmosphere in all of our homes should be one of respect and love.

RESPECTING CHILDREN

I love the way my husband treats our children. They are valuable people to him. When they talk, we both stop and listen. Even the two-year-old, who sometimes has long pauses in the middle of his sentences as he tries to remember his words, gets our uninterrupted attention while he is talking. "I...are...am...want to dwink, dwink water, ina tup (cup). Ina barfwoom, ina tap."

We have our family dinner at 6pm. The evening routine starts at 5pm, with tidy-up time, followed by bath-time at 5:30pm, and then we sit down to eat at 6pm. (The baby eats at 5pm, before his bath, and then sits in his highchair at the table with us, with a toy or two, while we eat.) On the few occasions when Daddy has had to miss family dinner or leave in a hurry to get to an evening meeting, he always apologises to the children and asks them to please excuse him. They know that they are very important people in his, and our, lives, and that they are worthy of being spoken to with respect.

One evening I phoned my husband to see if he was on his way home, because the children were waiting to play cricket with him. He was planning to run an errand on his way, but hearing that his VIP's were waiting for him, he changed his plan, and rushed straight home. Later, when they were bathing, he nipped out again to the shops as he had planned to do earlier. I love that these little people are important enough for him to inconvenience himself in order to show courtesy to them by not keeping them waiting.

Don't get me wrong, they know the world doesn't revolve around them. Being in a family of five kids, that lesson is a built-in reality already! But they know how to treat each other with respect because they have been treated that way themselves by the parents they are modeling their lives on.

I am proud of my man, that although he is a pastor and is loving people and listening to them all day long, and sometimes all night, he still has time to stop and listen when his VIP's are talking.

Speaking respectfully

I think respect needs to come before discipline. A child needs to know that they are valued and that they count. Coming back to my reason for writing this book - that is to explore ways that our parenting can be an accurate portrait of God and the way He is with His children - it is essential to capture in our parenting the love and value that God gives to each one of us.

I have been bedridden due to an injury while writing parts of this book, and my parenting style during this time leaves me wanting to encourage all of you NOT to do what I am having to do. All I can hear in my house is myself shouting out instructions to my children from my room.

"Kade (1), get up off the floor and ask nicely! Tantrums are not allowed."

"Jed (5), play gently with your little brother! You'll hurt him if you do that!"

"Rourke (3), share nicely!"

"Rich (my husband), have you given Kade his antibiotics this morning?"

Etc, etc, etc. It's awful. When I give instructions to my children, and particularly when I discipline them, I prefer to do it discretely and respectfully. It is so much less obtrusive, when you are in a public place or someone else's home, to speak at a volume that doesn't dominate the conversation in the room. If it only affects one person, then only their attention needs to be gotten.

More importantly, I find it disrespectful when my children yell for me rather than coming to speak to me face-to-face and I would like to afford them the same respect. It is unnecessarily embarrassing for them to be reprimanded for all to hear, and I think that honouring our children is an essential ingredient to fair discipline. The other extreme to avoid is speaking under our breaths with clenched teeth - that can be just as destructive.

I enjoy living in a home where people speak gently and respectfully to one another, and where the atmosphere is peaceful and pleasant. I think the 'lady' of the home should set an example of gentle speech.

When God has pointed out my errors, I have found Him always to do it in a private moment that leaves me feeling loved and well-guided – and positively grateful! True, it has, on occasion, come through a person and the human messenger, most often, adds a bit of his or her own sting to it. But when I take what they have said before the Lord, He lovingly confirms the truth of what they have said and I feel excited and motivated to change. If our parenting is going to bring God glory and be a picture of Him and His parenting style to our children and to observers, then it needs to illicit the same reaction in our children.

Respecting Their Pride

The other day our six year old daughter came through to us, after the girls had been put to bed in the room that they share, to report a problem. She was a bit hesitant, not knowing whether she and her sister would be punished for still being awake, but needing our help nonetheless.

"Um... Jada needs your help... she's tied herself in a knot and can't get free..."

Well, we burst out laughing and she smiled in relief that we were not going to punish them immediately. We went through to find that Jada had her knee up to her nose, and had wrapped a ribbon around her neck and under her knee, and tied a knot that had tightened with the weight of her leg pulling on it, and was now impossible to undo. The ribbon was wound too tightly to be able to slip her head or her leg out of it, so we ended up having to get scissors to cut it off.

But before we did that, we thought an apt punishment would be to take a photo of her on my husband's phone and joke that we would post it on facebook. We thought that would be a mild and appropriate discipline - but we were very wrong. She was so upset and cried inconsolably at the prospect of being humiliated.

My husband was amazing. He gathered her in his arms and assured her that we would only ever celebrate her successes in a public forum and never advertise her failures. We would protect her and never intentionally humiliate her. He explained that we were only joking about putting on facebook how she had gotten herself into a bind.

Our darling pre-teen cried even more in relief and it took another little while before we could settle them back into bed. (And just to let you know, I did ask her before sharing this story, and she was quite happy for me to share it.) Respecting our children needs to include protecting them from humiliation.

Respecting Their Time

The world does not revolve around our children - we know that. Children are a blessing, and need to fit into the other important aspects of our lives and our purpose. It is important not to bring your life to a halt because you have a baby, and to continue to be a part of your community, your church, your family, your marriage and your friendships.

That being said, I think we need to also consider our children when we are rushing around to hundreds of parties, family gatherings, meetings, dinners and functions. We need to be aware of how they are doing and their ability to cope with the demands on them. A child needs to have sufficient sleep, sufficient quiet alone-time and sufficient attention in order to flourish.

When we stop to think about the innumerable things we want our children to learn, and be equipped for, and experience, while they are still under our care, it tends to give us a sense of urgency about managing their time, and making the most of the hours and days and years that we have with them.

Respecting Their Privacy

Is a mother reading her daughter's secret diary disrespectful? Should children be allowed to close their bedroom doors? If a child has a friend over to play should you hover around, or give them some privacy? Is there a certain age that a child should be allowed a cell-phone or an email/facebook account, without their parents checking every message that is received and sent?

These are interesting questions and I'm sure our answers will be quite varied. In a seemingly ambiguous case like this, when I have read and received conflicting advice, I will tend to go back and think about how God parents us. It seems to me that God is not big on privacy. He's big on living in the light and having your deeds known. He's big on knowing us and on keeping us accountable. He sees the things that are done in secret, and He tells us to confess our sins to men, because, to quote a dear pastor friend of ours, "Confession breaks the obsession".

So God 'knows' us because He loves us. However, I have never heard of God snooping around to find out whether we've been good or bad. God is quite clear that He is light and that nothing can be hidden from him. He never goes behind our backs to illicit information.

My children are well informed that it is my job to protect them and to guide them in their choices. They know exactly what I mean when I talk about living in the light. It is not something to be afraid of or to be threatened by. I am not watching and waiting to see if they will make a mistake, but I can help them when they are starting to think or act in a way that will become detrimental for them or their relationships. They feel safe in that knowledge.

That being said, I think there comes a time in a child's life when they would prefer to change their clothes in private, or even to have some moments alone to think or read or pray. My children understand that those privacies are a reward that they receive for being trustworthy. Privacy is not a right, but it can be awarded to people who are able to handle it with integrity, not giving in to temptations to do things 'in the dark' or behind closed doors.

It is not a matter of age, but rather of protection. Many of the men I know, including my husband, have their internet usage emailed automatically to a friend of theirs, so that they can easily resist any possible temptation to use the internet for clandestine purposes. My husband is free to check my phone at any time he likes - I don't find it intrusive, but rather protective, and I will do the same for him.

So, as far as privacy goes with children, I would say that yes, respect is still essential, but so is teaching them the privilege of being open and accountable.

It is definitely a privilege that they can understand, and make the most of. Many times a child of mine has come to me because they feel tempted, and they want me to help them before they give in to their temptation.

"Mommy, please can you put those crunchies where I can't reach them because I feel like I want to take one."

What a privilege it is to partner with them in their desire for righteousness.

I think the more we treat our children with respect, the more they deserve it. Besides that, they do not belong to us but to God, and are only given to us to care for for a short while. Let us always remember that we are only stewarding what is His, and parent these children with fear and trepidation!

CHILDREN RESPECTING ADULTS

We had a not-so-funny comedy of errors at home one evening. I had just got home from a few days in Jo'burg for work, and was on the bed with my five children, being showered with gifts of homemade jewelry, scribbled pictures and misspelled love letters, when my fourteen month old baby started to vomit. Unfortunately I was home alone with them, so I told the other kids not to move or touch any mess, and rushed to the bathroom with my baby. Silly me - I forgot to think that bath-time earlier in the evening, without Mom's supervision, had been a splash-a-thon, and as I ran into the bathroom, I slipped and did the splits and landed on the floor, pukey baby and all!

There I lay, seven-months pregnant and moaning in agony, my baby next to me covered in vomit and crying, devastated at being dropped by his mommy. My children came rushing into the bathroom. My six and nine year old girls were trying to help through their tears, and my five year old boy was choked up and asking me if the baby in my tummy was going to die. The three-year-old took one look at everyone and burst into tears.

I could feel the baby moving strongly and I wasn't bleeding, so after a long, painful hour of cleaning up, resettling everyone into bed (where they had been before I arrived home, thanks to my amazing friend who had been babysitting), and dealing with a few more vomiting episodes from my baby, I finally lay down and went to sleep. I awoke shortly after, as pregnant woman do, to go to the loo, only to find I couldn't move!

It was a long and painful night, not least of all because of the unborn baby dancing on my full bladder, before I could get hold of my husband in Cape Town to ask for help. We established that I couldn't get from my bed to the doctor any other way than on a stretcher, so we ordered an ambulance, much to the delight of my children!

It turned out that I had torn my front and back hip joints (the pubic symphysis and right sacroiliac), I couldn't walk or sit, but had to spend the next few weeks lying on my bed, only barely able to roll over. Often, when we are unable to serve our children the way we want to, due to having a pregnant tum, or a newborn babe, or even an injury or illness, we feel guilty. A friend of mine wisely taught me that a season of weakness or illness in a mom is a wonderful opportunity for the children to learn how to love and serve. Often a mom will put her own needs aside for the sake of her family, but in doing so, she can unwittingly teach her children to take her for granted. While a mom might be ok with that, what's not ok is the fact that, who the children are at home, is who they are - i.e. unless they are taught to think about their mother's needs, they are unlikely to think about putting anyone else's needs above their own either. Putting aside your own desire to serve your children, and allowing them moments and seasons of learning to love and serve you, is not something to feel guilty about, but actually a loving and essential part of growing and developing our children.

That brought comfort to me during the following few weeks, as my daughters made me tea and helped out with the little ones and my sons brought me my food before sitting to enjoy their own. My precious three year old boy would even help me after a shower by drying between my toes and helping me thread my feet into my pants - which was rather challenging as he was still learning to put his own undies the right way around! Those weeks were made easier as I was encouraged that I was still doing my job as a mom, and intentionally molding my children's characters. My older children were already a blessing, but I noticed a huge difference in my three-year-old, who was home with me every day, and helped me with countless requests to pass me things, or pick things up off the floor, or do something for his one year old brother. Even my fourteen-month-old adapted to my limitations and would oblige me by following simple instructions. As I relearned how to walk, he was so sweet in helping me move my walking frame forward a few inches, and then waiting for me to take a step. It was so precious!

The wonderful gift that we give our children when we allow them to put our needs first sometimes, is that they realise that there are other people in the world who have needs, too. The best people to learn that on is their mommies and daddies whom they love so much.
My husband has been instrumental in teaching our children this lesson. I have often overheard conversations like this:
"Dad, can I please have the wing of the chicken?"
"Let's just wait and ask Mom what she wants first and then we'll see what's left, ok?"
And I think that's lovely. Similarly, when my husband is sleeping or working, I will make sure that the children mind him and are considerate in playing quietly. This respect and consideration needs to be afforded to the whole family.

My mum was apparently unusual in her thoughtfulness when we were growing up. When we were teenagers, if we were sleeping in late in the morning on the weekend or holidays, she would always keep the house really quiet, even postponing vacuuming until later when we had woken up. Most people I mention that to are surprised, because their mothers wouldn't allow them to sleep in, in an effort to teach them not to be lazy. But I think what my mum did was right - she understood that growing teenagers need extra sleep, and she showed us her love by accommodating our needs. That being said, we were not being inconsiderate teenagers and staying up all night playing video games! Obviously we also had to be reasonable enough to fit into the family routine.

Starting Young

Don't you just hate it when your baby yells at you? Somehow, it doesn't matter that they are only small and unable to talk yet - it is still awful when they yell for everything they want, throw food and toys back at you that they don't want, and generally be quite abusive! (That is said tongue-in-cheek, because I guess 'abusive' is a bit strong... but I sure feel abused after being kicked in the stomach, having my hair pulled out and being yelled at.)

My baby has just turned one. I definitely think that we can start being a bit more demanding of him and his manners. I learnt an amazing thing from a really good mommy friend of mine who is a few years ahead of me. When I was still single, I used to visit Jacqui for tea, mostly just to glean from her wisdom, and I was surprised one day at the calm way she spoke to her fifteen month old boy when he was shouting at her. He needed help climbing onto a rock in the garden so he started to moan. Jacs just said to him, "Don't talk to Mommy like that. If you need help, ask nicely." I was astounded when he changed his tone of voice. His words were still unintelligible, but he made a noise that sounded like a gentle request and pointed at the rock he wanted to climb. She jumped up and lifted him onto it and he carried on playing.

Now, after witnessing that, certainly by the age of twelve months, but probably from a few months earlier, I start to demand good manners from my babies. When he throws his food or toys, he gets a stern but gentle, "No throwing toys," as well as a wag of the finger so he knows I mean business and am not just talking in a funny voice for his entertainment.

When he yells to be up, I say, "Up, Mama" in the way I want him to ask so he can start learning how I would like to be spoken to by him. When he shouts frustratedly for a toy someone else has or for food I am being too slow on delivering, I say, "Ta?" so he can learn to ask nicely. As he shows more understanding, so I will hold back from picking him up or giving him what he wants until he has asked appropriately... that should be in the next month or so. Already he has stopped pulling my hair out its roots if I remind him to be "gentle with mommy", and show him how to stroke gently.

He loves to learn and is pleased when he figures out how I want him to behave and treat me, and his toys etc. He loves to be praised and to get things right. It is amazing how much they understand and can manage if we raise our expectations of them. It doesn't take long before they realise how to ask, just like my friend's little boy had learnt. They try with a moan or a cry, we remind them to ask nicely, and they say something in their sweetest tone of voice like, "Mama?", or "Help me?", or "Ta?".

So hopefully soon, my day will feel a little less like I have just run the gauntlet... until the next baby finds his strength and his voice before he finds his manners!

Valuing Words

Have you ever given your children an instruction, only to find that it was not followed through with? They get home from school and you ask them to unpack their lunch boxes, but come that evening when you're making lunches for the next day, you look in the cupboard, and the sink, and the dishwasher, and you can't find it anywhere. Obviously, it was never taken out of the bag.

Respect in our house includes valuing the words that are spoken by a person. I have told my children, "When I speak, you need to show that you think I'm important and special by listening and hearing what I say. If you didn't hear nicely, or you can't remember what I said, then ask me straight away, 'Sorry, Mummy, I know you asked me to do something, but I can't remember what it was. Please can you tell me again?' If you just forget what I have said, or don't listen to me, that is disrespectful." And as I will address in a later chapter, 'disrespect' my kiddies know, means discipline.

Similarly, my husband and I make sure they know that we value their words, too. If we're in the middle of something, like changing a nappy with a screaming baby kicking at us, and one of our children launches into a play-by-play of their day at school, we'll say, "My darling, I really want to hear your story but I can't listen right now, so can you wait and tell me later?" We teach them that they need to wait until we are looking into their eyes, and then they know that they have our attention

When we call our children from the next room, we expect them to answer us and come running immediately. Very often, though, when we call them, they know it's because they've been doing something naughty! So instead of coming running, they rather just quickly stop what they've been doing and hope that will satisfy us! But it is important to insist that they are both obedient, and respectful, and that they do learn to come running through with a "Yes, Mum?".

Just this afternoon, my son and I played a game to reinforce this. Well, to be honest, I was trying to avoid giving him a smack, which was not very consistent of me because he knew he deserved one for not coming straight away. So instead of spanking him I said, "Let's try that again... Go back to your room and I'll give you another chance."

I called and he came very slowly and reluctantly.

"Nope, that would still get a smack. Let's try again."

I called and he appeared quickly with a "Yes, Mum?", but only just poking his head around the corner.

"Almost," I said. "But you need to run straight to me, not just poke you head around, and don't forget to call 'Coming!' so I know you're on your way."

Third time lucky, I called his name and he said "Coming!" and quickly ran into my room and said "Yes, Mum?"

"That's it, my boy! No smack for you! And remember to do that next time so you don't have to get a smack."

Greeting respectfully

A culture of respect in the home needs to include warm and loving greetings between the family members. In this area, it is helpful to remember that love is a choice, not necessarily a feeling. Sometimes we are not in the mood to be affectionate, and in some cases we may go through a period of years where this is the case. But what an incredible gift we give when we teach our children that love, and even affection, is a choice. In deed, it is even a responsibility in a family relationship as a means of showing respect.

Children should not be allowed to walk past their parents in the morning without greeting them warmly. When they come home from school, or arrive at the home, they should be taught to seek out their parents to say hello. They should even be taught to ask after their parents' days and take an interest in others.

Remember, we are parenting with an end product in mind, and teaching our children about affection in a relationship, and considering how to make other people feel special in a greeting will stand them in excellent stead for their own marriages later on. Many marriages have disintegrated because affection waned... but teaching our children that love is a choice - an action after which feelings will follow again - might well save their marriages one day.

Interrupting

Kids are notorious for interrupting, and it is seldom ever in disobedience. More likely it is in excitement, or perceived emergency, or just because their world still revolves entirely around themselves. It is not something that should annoy us, and definitely not embarrass us, no matter who we are busy in conversation with. We just need to constantly remind them to see the situation that is beyond their own and remind them what we expect of them.

I ask my children to stand quietly next to me or put their hand on my arm (or leg if they're little and I'm standing) if they want my attention. I acknowledge their request by putting my hand over theirs until there is a break in the conversation, and I can listen to their request.

If they can see that I am in the middle of something, like reading or speaking on the phone, or concentrating on a task, I ask that they wait until I am finished, or else ask me if they can talk to me before launching into their request or tale.

Respecting Closed Doors

Privacy is an area where parents and children are not equal. Everybody needs to be accountable, and to live 'in the light', yes, but children are not the people to whom parents must be accountable!

The parents' bedroom door is most certainly allowed to be closed on occasion, for many reasons. I mean, you never know, they could be wrapping gifts!

In our home, for many years now, my husband and I have had to get by on very little sleep. We've been in the baby phase for over seven years! Our sleep and rest times are extremely precious, and our patience is severely tested when we are woken up unnecessarily by older children who could have waited a little longer before asking for what they want.

For this reason, we are constantly reminding them that our closed door needs to be respected. Not only should they not enter without knocking, but they should not knock unless there is an emergency that requires immediate attention.

Like all lessons for young children, we remind them often of our expectations, as well as going over various scenario's of what does and does not constitute a reasonable excuse for an interruption.

This way, our precious sleep is somewhat protected, as well as our stolen moments of intimacy... to wrap gifts, and such.

CHILDREN RESPECTING SIBLINGS

I was wanting to share a story to illustrate how children who respect one another are able to enjoy each other's company, but so many precious memories came to mind that I was unable to choose. We were on a week's retreat at a timeshare resort in the mountains at the time, and that afternoon, they were dancing on the lawn together in a thunderstorm. That morning, the stronger bike riders were teaching the weaker riders so that they wouldn't feel left out when they were riding around the resort. I could tell stories of them building forts in the lounge, and playing soccer on the lawn. They play school-school together, and even have fun throwing rotten tomatoes at each other!

To avoid these games ending in tears, or to encourage our children to want to play together, we need to teach them to respect one another. I am convinced that good, intentional parenting can minimise and even avoid the constant sibling bickering that parents seem to have resigned themselves to accepting.

> Good, intentional parenting can minimize sibling fighting.

Of course, our children will have different personalities and enjoy some different activities. It is a given that there will be times that the older ones will want to play without the younger ones, or the boys will want to play without the girls, but when these preferences are handled with respect and kindness, they need not cause hurt.

Sibling fighting can cause such a build up of resentment over the years that relationships can be damaged and personalities formed around these hurts.

Speaking Politely

One of the most consistent rules in our home, and an area of little tolerance, is the way we all speak to one another. Our children are not expected to speak to us in one way, but permitted to speak to each other in another way. They must afford each other, even those younger than them, dignity and honour in their speech. This has to start at the top. My husband and I can not speak to one another any differently than we would speak to a friend, or a boss, or whoever else is worthy of preferential treatment. Similarly, we need to speak to our children in a manner that acknowledges that they are, in fact, God's children, and worthy of honour and respect. Children are NOT there so that we can take out our frustrations on them, and feel satisfied by talking down to them in the way we wish we could talk down to some of the annoying adults in our lives.

When we fail, and most of us do, we need to be quick to apologise to our children, or to our spouses. I have often been heard to say, "My child, I'm sorry I spoke to you like that. What you were doing is not allowed, and you will still be disciplined for it, so that I can teach you not to do that again. But I didn't need to speak to you like that. It was disrespectful and you deserve to be spoken to nicely. Please forgive me."

When your standards for yourself are high, then you can also ask that your children treat each other with respect. You can legitimately say, "Am I allowed to speak to you like that? Then you also don't speak to your brother/sister like that."

Imitation is everything in this area. If a child is not playing by the rules and not listening to the others, then you discipline them by teaching them, saying, "My baby, if you don't listen nicely then you can't play with the others. If you want a turn, say, 'Please can I have a turn after you?'" When your children are trying to solve the same problem on their own, they will use the same words: "Boy, if you're not listening then you don't get to play with us. Ask nicely and we will give you a turn."

When you help your children to understand one another it can be very helpful in teaching them to be patient with one another. Explain to the girls why boys do certain things. Explain to the five-year-old why the three-year-old behaves in a certain way. Explain to the math's genius why the creative one is making certain decisions. Help them to be proud of one another and recognise each other's strengths. Teach them to praise one another.

Help them to recognise each other's weaknesses or as yet undeveloped characters, and to understand why

> Help your children to be patient with each other by explaining to them their siblings' age-limited capabilities.

those younger than them are not as good at sharing, or keeping up. Discipline those areas in love and understanding, so that your children can have the same attitude as you towards each other's failings - that they are just areas that are still being worked on, and not malicious actions that should be taken personally.

It is impossible for us to cover every area of sibling contention, but if we hold up all our children's dealings with one another against the standard of respect then we will have a good idea how each situation needs to be dealt with.

Perhaps the most important key to curbing sibling rivalry is spending enough time loving our children and praising them for their little milestones and achievements. If each of them are swimming in affection and confidence, then the need to compete against one another in an unhealthy way is minimised You will find your children doing the same thing:

"Wow, look, Mom, Kiara can dive!"

"Well done, Jed, you're such a fast rider."

"Look, look, Kade is walking! He's such a clever boy!"

Parenting requires a lot more training than disciplining. Be constantly coaching your children in the way to treat people well.

"Mom, can I go and play with the others?"

"Sure, just ask them nicely if you can play with them."

As one is coming to help the other to carry something heavy, prompt them quietly:

"Say, 'Thank you, my darling sister.' "

> **Parenting requires a lot more training than disciplining.**

Don't allow your children to ignore one another when they are being spoken to. Particularly when the little one is trying to participate in a game, his pleas tend to go unanswered. I have to remind my children often to answer each other when they talk. I don't want to let the small things slide because I want them all to learn how to value each other, and to experience that they are valued by each other. They are playing with princes and princesses of the kingdom of God, and I remind them of that often.

Sharing

From when they are babies, our children need to learn to ask for things with an open hand to receive - this simple gesture will help them to understand the difference between asking and snatching. It is no good asking for something when you already have your hand grasped around it. An open palm puts the power in the hand of the one being asked - and they are far more likely to share willingly when it is their own decision.

My oldest four kids were sitting in a tight circle on the trampoline as I was writing this, shoulder-to-shoulder to protect their snack from our dogs. I had given them one platter to share, and on it were eight Provita's, four Marie biscuits, four banana's and a pile of raisins. I love giving them one platter to share because, for starters, it means less washing for me! But also, I think it's good for their math's skills, as well as their sharing skills. Of course, the biscuits and banana's are simple math's and shouldn't cause a problem. The pile of raisins is more challenging, because they all love raisins, and they are each going to have to not be greedy so they will all get some.

I think it is essential to give our kids the opportunity to share. It seems these days all the kiddies treats are individually packaged, so parents can dish them out fairly. If I am buying a treat, I will buy one big packet of chips, not four or five little ones. My children have learnt that they need to share politely, because anyone who is snatching or grabbing has to give back what they have snatched, and possibly forfeit the rest of the treat.

I have found that people often try and protect children from having to share (in an effort to prevent arguments?). They will want to give each child the same gift so that they won't fight. They will kindly offer to send extra party treats home with me for my other children so that the child who attended the party won't have to share their 'party pack'.

I prefer to give them opportunities to share. If they're offered toys at the Wimpy we take different ones, so that they can learn to swop and timeshare the toys. Sweets brought home from school or parties are shared with joy. It delights them to be the one in charge of dishing out their sweets or toys and sharing them between themselves. It is a feeling of power, and as their siblings are so grateful, and Mom and Dad are commending them, they have decided that it really is more blessed to give than to receive.

RESPECTING OTHERS OUTSIDE THE HOME

A family home is a fantastic place to learn manners, and being able to introduce our kids to other people outside of our family is a great test. Teaching our children to respect others is very much a case of imitation. Social and friendly parents are likely to produce children after their own kind. Explain to them why you are choosing to exercise certain manners and courtesies so that they can learn the value and reason behind being socially considerate.

Greeting

Most kids are not very fond of greeting people. Either they are too shy, or else they are just too busy. To have to stop and take notice of someone who is greeting them is very inconvenient. It seems an unnecessary thing to have to do, particularly when it leaves them feeling either embarrassed, or, at least, put out.

However, if we change the focus onto the 'other' people, and explain to our children how a warm greeting can leave a person feeling loved and welcomed, we begin to speak their language. When my children have heard that when they ignore someone, or greet them reluctantly, it leaves that person feeling left out and lonely, it motivates them to overcome their reluctance.

> When your children fall short, it doesn't mean you have failed, it just means you're not yet finished!

A warm and heartfelt greeting needs to be broken down for our children to understand it. They need to look into people's eyes, they need to smile and be friendly, they need to use the person's name, and if they can't remember it, then listen out for Mom to prompt them.

When caring for other people is the reason for greeting them well, shyness is no excuse. I am totally ok for children to be shy and to feel a need to cling to mommy's skirt sometimes. But it is not a reason to be unkind, and it is not a reason to be unfriendly.

Children need to be taught to stand up and greet someone who walks into the room, and acknowledge their presence. They do not always have to wait to be greeted. Also, we need to show our children, by example as well as by teaching, that all people are worthy of being greeted, irrespective of social or financial standing.

Consideration of Others

My husband has an extraordinarily high level of consideration for others. When he drives through a residential area at night, he keeps his lights on dim so that they won't shine through people's windows! When we have the privilege of holidaying at a resort or dining at a restaurant, he is constantly telling our children to talk quietly so as not to disturb other holiday makers or diners around us. It drives me mad, because I hate being shushed - it just takes all the wind and excitement out of a good story! But, to be honest, I love that he has taught me more about thinking of others, and that together we can bring up our children in the same way.

I had a friend who was incredibly thoughtful and considerate - she was always worried about how she might be putting others out. She's the kind of guest you love to have in your home because they leave it even tidier than when they arrived.

Her little boy was two or three years old when I knew her and she was really struggling to take him out of their home or to be a part of any 'Mom's Group', because she felt so uncomfortable with his noise levels and was constantly worried about him being a disruption.

The trouble was, she was also very sensitive towards saying 'No' and shushing her little boy the whole time, and so she decided it would be easier to allow him to stay at home, where he could do what he wanted without being restricted by having to consider those around him. That way she wasn't putting him 'out' either.

I encouraged her that, although it was great that she was considerate of her boy and wanted to afford him the same respect that she had for others, it was also important not to deny him the privilege of learning from her how to be respectful of others. While it is true that her son's activity would be restricted by her high standards of consideration, he would also turn out to *have* her high standards!

Manners Give Them a Head Start

It is our responsibility as parents to teach our children good manners. If you have not been given that privilege yourself, or feel that there is more to good manners than what you know, then you need to take the initiative to get a book and read up on it, so that you can teach your children.

Society judges people on their manners, and if we are going to bring up our children to be world changers, and leaders, and to have influence over people, then we need to help them get their foot in the door by having good manners.

A friend of ours was being considered for a management position in a global company, and after the interviewees were taken out for dinner, he was awarded the job on the basis of his exceptional table manners. Another friend was wanting to marry a young lady, but at first sight did not seem to the parents to 'look' right for their daughter. However, after a single meeting in their home, he won them over by his outstanding manners, and was given their blessing to marry their daughter. A third friend, though on paper he appeared to be husband material, was rejected as a son-in-law because he didn't seem to know how to treat a lady with gentlemanly manners.

Manners matter, and we can set our children up for success by giving them the skill of knowing which manners to apply in which circumstances. And remember, your children are still in training, so their manners are not to be criticised, but coached.

Manners Put Others First

When people are gathering in our home, we teach our children to offer their chairs to adults... but why is that? It is important for our children to understand the reason behind what they are being asked to do, lest they think that we value them less than our guests.

To begin with we need to show them that the bible teaches us in Philippians 2:3-4 to "Do nothing out of selfish ambition or vain conceit, but in humility, consider others better than yourselves. Each of you should look not only to your own interests, but also to the interests of others." Not that everyone else is superior, but as Christians we choose to give others preferential treatment. This is not just a child-adult thing, but something that everybody needs to be doing. Point out to them how the men offer their chairs to ladies, and how the adults offer their chairs for the elderly. Help them to notice when special care is offered for people who are disabled or pregnant. In this way, the children feel included to be offering their place for others, rather than left out and undervalued just because they are young.

Make an effort to teach your children how manners differ in different cultures. Besides being fascinating and educational, it is serves to be helpful in making them aware of manners in our own culture. Have Chinese dinners and let them try their hand at chopsticks!

When we have the privilege of entertaining guests from other cultures we whisper in our children's ears as to how we are going to accommodate our guest and make them feel welcome. Often we will ask our guest to explain manners and customs from their culture or the countries that they have visited. We've learned that in countries that use chopsticks, it is more polite to stretch at the table, because to ask someone to pass you a dish is an inconvenience, as they have to release their grip on their chopsticks. We've learned how in some cultures it is polite to bring a gift when visiting peoples homes, whereas in others it would be a slight on the host's ability to provide.

When we were away once, and our housekeeper was with us, we managed to convince her to eat dinner with us one evening. We were having a braai and we told our children at the table that they were welcome to eat with their hands. Afterward, we explained to them that we had specifically given them that option so that our guest would feel comfortable to eat in the same manner that she did at her home.

Conversely, I remember my shame when once I saw my children, who were eating dinner at a little kiddies' table, using their hands instead of their forks. I reprimanded them, saying, "Do you think you're savages?" and then cringed with embarrassment, both because our Zulu housekeeper was in earshot, and because I had just implied a terrible condescension on hundreds of other cultures. I tried to quickly dig myself out of a hole by explaining to them that in our home we used these particular table manners, which they needed to follow.

I always remember the story so fondly, of the Queen of England entertaining a foreign guest. When he, in ignorance, drank the water from out of the finger bowl that had been set in front of him to wash his hands in, she proceeded to do the same, in order to make him feel at ease. That story delights me, because it captures the epitomy of manners. We learn manners in order to know how to be considerate of others, and how to make them feel at home with us, and how to be respectful in their homes. We do NOT learn manners so that we can be set apart and more 'cultured' than other people. The worst manners in the world is, ironically, to criticise someone else's manners. Our manners are learned so that we can include people, not exclude them.

When a Taiwanese refuses to finish his meal, but leaves a little to show that he has been served sufficient; when an Australian refuses to disrespect a woman by opening her car door and thus insinuating weakness on her behalf, but will graciously wash all the dinner dishes and make his bed; when a Zulu boy pushes in front of his teacher when walking through the door to the classroom in order to make sure that it is safe for her to enter; we need to appreciate the reason for the action, rather than criticising the difference to our particular manners.

> The person with the best manners is not the one who knows the most rules, but the one who makes others feel the most welcome.

The person with the better manners is not the one who knows the most rules, and measures others against them, but the one who expects 'manners' only from himself, and learns every way to 'value others more highly' than himself.

5 LOVING ON PURPOSE

I heard a story many years ago that shaped my thoughts on parenting. Please forgive me for my memory if you've heard the original, and excuse my lack of reference to the source. The story goes something like this:

A woman asked to meet with a friend of hers to discuss her difficulties with her teenager. The friend agreed, as long as the woman was willing to have the conversation on a little boat out at sea. She had plans to go whale watching that day.
The troubled mother was pouring out her heart when her friend interrupted to point out a whale surfacing. She turned, but was too late to see it. The mother continued with her tale of how her teenager never talked to her, and how they were drifting apart, and how impossible he was to understand. A few minutes later, the friend saw the whale surfacing again, a little further on, but again the mother missed it.

After this happened a third time, the mother telling the tale complained, "Why do I always miss seeing this whale? It's always coming up in a different spot!"

At this, her friend explained, "Whale watching is a bit like parenting. We're never quite sure when they're going to pop up. But if we're patient, we'll be there in the right place when they're exposed and vulnerable. The trick is to be observant and patient - before long you'll start to recognise the path they're on and be able to predict where they'll pop up next. Most importantly, when we do have the opportunity to see them and they're vulnerable, we need to make sure we don't take a shot at harpooning them! That is certain to ensure they'll never pop up again when you're around if they can help it!

I just love the concept of observant and intentional parenting. Gosh, to think of it, God is amazing in the way that He *sees* each person. There are countless stories, both in the bible, as well as around us, of God noticing small details in people's lives.

A dear friend of mine was relaying to me how she had put her dishwasher on before church, and for some odd reason, felt prompted by God that it was not a good idea. Dismissing the voice, as it seemed an unreasonable warning, she continued to put it to work. Getting home from church a few hours later, she found her kitchen flooded, and had to acknowledge that God was interested in every menial detail of her life, even if she was going to ignore Him!

We remember the story of Hannah, a precious lady outcast by her friends and society for being barren, crying out to God for a child. God sees her and cares, and takes time to understand the hurts in her heart, and is good enough to grant her what she desires. (Samuel 1)

I think one of my favourite stories of all time is found in Genesis 21:8-21. A servant woman is treated cruelly but God sees. This woman is made to lie with her master on his wife's behalf, in order to produce an heir for them. However, years later, when her master and his wife are blessed with their own natural heir, the servant girl and her son are kicked out and sent into the desert to die. This woman has no expectation that she is worth anything in society and her son has been produced outside of God's plan and yet God hears the boy's cries and sees them in the desert. He surprises her by showing that He is aware of her situation, and has been watching her life all along. He not only gives her and her son life, but tremendous blessings and promises as well.

God also has so much time for us. He has even gone to great lengths to make sure that nothing hinders us from being able to approach Him at any moment and speak to Him about any subject. Though He had to go to hell and back to give us this privilege, yet He considered it worth it.

God knows us intimately, even to the point of knowing when each hair falls off our heads, because the bible says He keeps count (Matthew 10:30). And we thought it was sentimental to keep our baby's first curl!

If one of our chief purposes of being parents is to bring God glory by reflecting how He parents us, then we need to get this right. We need to be intentional about knowing our children. We need to observe them and make every effort to understand them. It might require studying psychology and reading books. It might require going on courses. It will definitely require a lot of watching, a lot of listening and a lot of time. And it will definitely require God's wisdom and insight.

> To imitate God with our parenting, we need to be observant and intentional about knowing our children.

Our children are all different, and, what's more, they're changing all the time. This is not something we get 'figured out'. For me, this is one of the most exciting parts of parenting. People often ask me if I feel unfulfilled because I am no longer using the professional degree that I studied. They ask if I don't miss using my brain in that way. I think that is such a limited view on parenting! At work, I had to master certain skills so that I would always deliver excellence. Once you're good at something, you have to keep doing it so that you're an asset to the company. Here at home, the work is way too challenging and diverse to get everything right all the time! I am constantly being stretched and tested and having to go back to the drawing board to come up with new methods of approaching different problems. I love it! It feels like I cracked the jackpot when my pre-teen understands in her heart what I've been trying to get through to her, or when I finally help my three-year-old to understand which colour is blue and which is green.

Love Days and Floor Days

A few weeks ago our family had been going through quite a busy period and the children had had to fit in with a demanding schedule, and experienced a bit of sidelining. Most of them seemed to be handling it pretty well, but we noticed our five year old son was playing up a little. He was sulking when being disciplined, and seemed to be quite sensitive. When his teacher was thoughtful enough to mention to us that he had refused to join in to an activity at school because of a lack of confidence in that particular ability of his, we knew he needed some positive attention.

I asked him if he would like to stay home from school and spend a day cuddling with me in bed and reading library books, and he jumped at the idea, so we knew we were on the right track. We chatted openly about him needing a 'love day' to fill up his love tank, and he had fun showing me throughout the day where on his body he thought his love tank was up to. By the evening he said it was up to his head and he was ready to go back to school.

Often with my older babies or toddlers when I see their discipline slipping I will take what I call a 'floor day' with them. I put aside hope of achieving any other work for that day, and instead of giving them toys to play with on the floor next to me, I get down and play with them. They have my complete attention, and I can help them to remember appropriate behaviour before they make mistakes. As they lift up a toy to throw it, I can remind them that we don't throw toys, or as they open their mouths to shout, I can remind them to ask Mommy nicely. On these days I usually find very little spankings are required because I am able to help them choose the correct behavior in time. However, obviously I will use them if necessary. By the end of the day, or even after just an hour or two, the baby is back on track and remembers what is expected of him. Then just a gentle reminder from across the room is enough to make him stop snatching or put down what he's about to throw.

When we are observing our children carefully, we can have a much more flexible approach to discipline, without losing credibility or compromising our consistency. We can be more confident in what we expect of them and what they are capable of. We need to watch carefully to have insight as to whether our children are being disobedient because they are rebellious, or just because they are tired. Not that being tired or sick is an excuse for disrespect or disobedience, but it can help us to ask less of them so we don't put them into a situation in which they will struggle to obey. We might avoid calling them out of their bedroom to greet somebody, or choose not to ask them to complete a task that they will manage better after a sleep.

> When we are observing our children carefully we can be more flexible with our discipline, without losing credibility and consistency.

Family Time

Special family times, like most good intentions, never seem to happen, or at least not regularly enough, unless they are worked into our weekly routines and diaries.

In our home, it's seven o'clock on a Friday night and our kids have us crawling around the lounge like lions on a hunt! I am the mommy lion, so I have to do all the hard work of prowling and pouncing, while my husband gets to be the lazy daddy lion, 'pretending' to sleep on the couch! Don't worry, I'll get him up in a minute, once I've caught the 'buck' and then he'll have to get down on all fours and pretend to rip it apart with his teeth. I'll use that time to curl up on the couch with my baby lions while we wait for Daddy to have his fill!

It all started about two years ago when we decided to implement a family night once a week - that's like a 'date-night', but for the whole family. (A necessary thing when our lives are so full of evening meetings and adult time.) Well, to be truthful, we were hoping it was going to be Family Movie Night, but after our kids got scared and cried during every movie we tried, including 'Bambi', 'Barbie and the 12 Dancing Princesses', 'Shrek' and everything other than Barney, we finally admitted defeat.

So, now it is Family Games Night. My husband is a preaching pastor, so Sunday is a work day for him - our rest day is taken from 6pm on Friday until 6pm on Saturday. It's a family day, and starts with a special dinner on Friday evening, followed by Family Games Night.

Last week, we played 'Restaurant, Restaurant'. Our eldest daughter was needing some extra revision on money math's, so we set up the game so she could be the cashier. The younger children served us a wonderful, albeit plastic, meal, and the only hitch was the approximately three-million paper peas that we had to pick up afterwards!

One of my favourite games nights is just sitting around telling stories. I love hearing the kids learning to make up their own stories. They have gotten the hang of it now, so they can go on forever - but we have one up on them, cause we have figured out that we should ask them before they start if they know how their story is going to end. Obviously, everything is a learning opportunity, so we are teaching them how to formulate a story by asking before they start: "Do you know who is going to be in your story?"; "Do you know where your story is going to happen?"; "Do you know how it's going to start/end?"; "Do you know what's going to happen in the middle?".

It's a great opportunity to share stories about your childhood. As my dad would say, "When I was a little girl like you...". How we would giggle at that line, every time. It's also a good time to reinforce lessons they're busy learning, like, "There once was a little boy who didn't tell the truth...". Of course, he got eaten by crocodiles!

They love playing 'grownup' board games like Snakes & Ladders, and Ludo. Personally, I don't love bending forward with a pregnant tummy to move a token every ten seconds, and it's VERY time-consuming, but it's good for counting, and adding, and turn-taking, and strategising, so we do it every now and again.

Sometimes we put an extra effort into planning something special, like the night we did 'MG's have Got Talent!' That was a great one - everybody had to come up with one to three items to enter into the talent competition. Daddy did juggling and a magic trick. Jed (5) made us all go outside because his talent was that he could bowl to himself - a rare talent in deed! We waited to see what exactly that meant, and when he threw up the cricket ball and batted it clear out the property, we were all in awe and yelled into the home video camera, "Jed's Got Talent!". We had a fun evening of ballet, piano, drumming, throwing and catching, and even a few steps from our baby who was just learning to walk.

Another special memory was made the night we all camped out on the verandah. We set out a few mattresses and made chocolate milkshakes, and then later read stories by torchlight and had a midnight feast. In the morning, the sun woke us up and we had tea and rusks. I think it's relevant to point out that because our children are mostly given non-extravagant things it makes a treat like being allowed tea and rusks that much more exciting. Treats are rare - that's what makes them treats.

And then Saturday is Pyjama Day (an idea borrowed from Mark & Grace Driscoll's home) - we just stay at home, if possible, and the kids usually play some spread-out game that takes all day and the whole house, as a tent home is set up in the lounge, and mommy's bed in the main room is America, and the rocking chair in the nursery is an aeroplane. My husband will sometimes play cricket or wrestle with the kids, but I usually try and use this day as a rest for myself, and tend to graciously decline when asked to play or read to them on this day. They are generally quite understanding, because they have had lots of love and attention for the rest of the week, and they actually enjoy feeling like they are helping me by letting me have time off. In fact, often, they will try to help where they can with each other, by washing the toddlers hands for me, or entertaining the baby for a few minutes. It makes them feel valuable and important to be a 'blessing to mom'.

This weekly quality time is really treasured by our kids, and they miss it when we are unable to do Family Night. There's not much better for them, than thinking that the 'King' and 'Queen' of their world are willing to get down (sometimes right down - hands and knees and bellies on the floor!) and play a kiddie game with them. That's knowing you are treasured!

6 PRACTICAL POINTERS

There are a couple of methods to parenting that I have found, when applied, can make things that much easier in our families. These are totally personal and I only share them in case they might be useful in your home. They are not biblical principles in themselves, but like most applications, there are principles to be found within them.

Routine

The first is routine. When a child brushes his teeth every single evening after dinner, he becomes unlikely to fight it. When a baby is strapped into his car seat every single time he goes in the car, irrespective of the fight he puts up, he resigns himself to the way things are. When children know that they need to hop on the loo before they go in the car, no matter whether they need to or not, they just do it. Routine makes kids obey more readily. Giving in to their whining one time in ten makes the whining go on for years unnecessarily.

Our evening routine has the kids scurrying into bed excitedly, as fast as they can, leaves the house peacefully tidy, and gives hubby and me relaxing evenings alone to chat, read, and love... shall I share how?

It starts at 5pm. (Our eldest child has one to one-and-a-half hours of homework, so that can be fitted in before this). So, five o' clock is tidy-up time. That includes me tidying what only I can tidy, and goes down age-appropriately. Each person doesn't tidy the mess they made, but rather the mess that they can manage to tidy effectively. So that means sometimes my two-year-old is tidying my mess by putting my shoes in the cupboard, and the four-year-old is tidying the two-year-old's mess by packing up the toys. We all work together because I have taught them that our house is a gift from God and we need to take care of it together to show that we appreciate it.

> Routine helps children to obey more readily.

Half past five is bath-time. All I want to say about bath-time, is that we all have to do it. I know it's hard work and it hurts your back, especially when you're pregnant, and your knees are bruised afterwards, and don't you just hate it when you are trying to get your toddler to step into his pants and he jumps up and head butts your chin?! I hear that there are some moms who love watching their kids splashing sweetly in the bath, and cherish getting them dressed into their cute little snuggly p.j.'s. But most of the time, for most of us, it is a physically demanding job at the end of a physically exhausting day. So picture moms around the world kneeling down and getting splashed when they weren't in the mood, and getting head butted in the chin too many times, and know that it's not long before we can say to our school kids, "Go and have a shower, honey. Don't forget to wash your hair, and come back all dressed with your slippers on, please!"

Six o'clock is supper time. Don't ask me when the cooking gets done... I guess doing as much prep as possible in the afternoon while it's 'outside play-time' helps. It depends if you have a second pair of hands/eyes to watch bath time... You might have to work that one out for yourself depending on how young your kids are, and if you can leave them unattended in the bath.

The table gets set during tidy-up time so it is all ready at six pm. Spoon-fed babies eat at five pm, before bath-time, and then they sit in their high chairs with some toys during dinner.

Now comes the clever part. Our supper is normally finished by about 6:25pm, so we have a rule, that if the children have done their teeth and wee's and are in bed by half past six, then they get story-time. If they dawdle, then they get a kiss and a cuddle, but no story. That has really worked for us, because instead of bed-time being a seven o'clock rush and us begrudging the extra kisses because we have a 7pm meeting, or TV programme to get to, we have a good half-hour to read, and chat through questions, and pray together. When we get the inevitable, "You never hugged me!" Or, "Please can you lie with me?" we don't have to be constantly telling our children, 'No'. We have time to 'cherish the moment' at bed-time.

Finally, and possibly the most important part of creating this perfect adult evening, is what happens after lights out (7pm). We have done a brave and infinitely rewarding thing. We have cancelled our TV subscription. It has had amazing consequences, but one of the best has been that my husband and I have an evening together, from 7pm, to catch up, swop diaries, share news, and even cuddle in bed and read together. It has had an obvious effect on our love life, and I am even getting around to reading a few classic novels. What young mom can say that? It's like 'date-night' every night!

So, that's our routine, and it works wonders for us. Maybe it will suit your family as well, and always remember, routines are made to be broken, so never say 'No' to life because you are stuck in a routine, but use it to give your home life stability.

Explain Expectations

Another very helpful trick to getting the best out of your children is letting them know what you expect from them before entering any situation. A good coach doesn't just bomb on his team after a bad game. He helps them to achieve success by prepping them for every possible scenario that might come up in the game.

> **Help them to achieve success by prepping them for possible scenarios.**

When I am parking at the shops, I will remind my kids what I expect of them for the next hour: "Now, remember, angels, what do we do in the shops? We stay close to Mommy. Keep your hands in your pockets or behind your backs. Don't nag me for anything. If I want to buy a treat for you I will, but I don't want you to ask for anything." (This is not a standard rule, but is helpful while grocery shopping!)

When we are arriving at someone's house I will remind them: "Remember, we are guests here so we need to respect their home and watch them to see what's allowed in this house. We need to say 'hello' with a friendly smile and look at the people's eyes. When Mommy says it's time to go, I want you to say, 'Yes, Mommy', and be grateful for the time we have had here."

Arriving at a family function, the conversation in our family bus might go something like this: "Listen up, everyone! We are going to be with Mommy's family now. The people's house we're going to are called Shar and Louis - do you remember them? That's Mommy's aunt and uncle, and they're special to me just like Uncle Tony or Auntie Cuttie are special to you. I want you to say 'hello' nicely to everyone because all the people here love you very much and they're our family." We'll continue to remind them of the various names and how they relate in the family, and make sure they're as prepared as possible to have a good time reuniting with family that they don't see everyday.

If we're going to an old person's house that is full of ornaments and not used to having children in it, we will make sure to explain that to them. If we're going to visit great-grannies that might be hard of hearing, or be likely to ask them the same question three or four times, we'll make sure they are expecting that, too. Obviously the exact instructions for each scenario will be variable and will depend on the particular manners we are trying to instill in them at the moment.

When we prepare our children sufficiently, we set them up for success, and negative discipline is needed less often. Conversely, when they do let us down, we can discipline them more confidently, knowing that we have given them a fair chance, and that they are acting out intentionally, not out of ignorance of the situation.

Keeping It Tidy

If you're anything like me, a disordered home is very unhelpful to your patience levels. When my home is out of control, I feel panicky, like I am not managing everything I need to, and my fuse is shorter than I need it to be. A third practical pointer that helps in making family life more pleasant, is learning how to organise your home.

Too often, I will have twenty people in my house and my husband will suggest that we move the couch, while everyone is watching, so we can all fit into the lounge in a circle. What will we find under there? And more importantly, how long will it have been there?

How, oh how, do we keep our houses tidy as moms of young children? I mean, as I walk from room to room tidying, my sweet children are following me, picking up random things, and putting them down in the next room. It's like shoveling snow while it's snowing!

Added to that, our lifestyle is such that we have people popping into our home at any random time, most of whom would not be as understanding as I would hope when they stand on a leftover peanut butter sandwich. They just don't get it that the sandwich is only from the last meal - it's not like it's been sitting there for days!

So how do we manage this mess?

To start off with, I think 'manage' is the operative word. We can't just tidy at the end of the day. It would take hours. I think we need to break it down into at least a three stage attack:

The first is how we play all day. Now, I know the toddler just redistributes random articles, so let's count him out. But as young as possible, the children need to be taught to play one thing at a time. So it goes, "Mom, can we ride bikes?"

"Sure, just put away the lego first."

But then, of course, it often goes, "But we're not finished with that game."

Don't feel bad. It's good for them to learn that a job needs to be finished and they can't just flit from one thing to the next and back again. It's good for task completion, and concentration, and sequencing, and a whole host of skills that they have listed on those pre-school term reports.

Secondly, we have tidy-up time before lunch, and again at the end of the day. This is a constant in the routine, which means the kids are expecting it and therefore don't moan. I have a nice looking basket in my living room, with four buckets in it labelled with each child's name. Throughout the day, when strange things, like socks, and toy cars, and hair-bands, make their way to the living room, I put them into the appropriate child's bucket, which keeps our living area respectable for pop-in visitors. Then at tidy-up time, they don't look around whining, "I don't know what to tidy." They just pick up their bucket and take it to their room and put things where they belong.

'Where they belong...' Are you thinking, "I wish they knew where things 'belonged'! If only!"? Very often, if they don't know where things belong, it's because you don't really know either. If you want your kids to tidy up well, you need to have a house that makes sense, and each thing needs to have a place. Re-organise their rooms so that they can tidy them. For example, if they are unable to stand books upright on a shelf, then let the books be in a pile in a box rather. Do a spring clean with them sometimes, and watch to see which things they are confused about where to tidy. Then either make a place for those things, or get rid of them!

I have loads of big plastic boxes. They are not cheap, but it brings me lots of peace and happiness to have an orderly house, so I reckon they're worth it! (Cue: Husband laughing at my plastic box obsession.) The boys' room has a box for cars, a box for figurines and plastic animals, a box for lego etc. The girls' room has a box for Barbies, a box for baby things, and a box each for their own 'special' things, like letters from friends, diaries, old birthday cards, and anything they want to keep that I don't have a spot for. Each room also has a basket for things that are lying around and need to be sorted later at tidy-up time, similar to my living room basket.

I have a three-tier vegetable rack where the top-tier is for completed kids drawings, the middle-tier is for drawings in progress, and the bottom-tier is for fresh paper. You get the idea. Everything has a place, or else it's out the house.

So, back to tidy-up time. They each tidy what I have put in their little buckets throughout the day, as well as looking around and tidying the house in general. At this stage, we all work together. Each person is not just responsible for their own mess, but they do whatever they can manage at their age. They have been taught that our house is a gift from God and that we need to take care of it to show that we appreciate it. I have explained to them that just as when they give me a flower they have picked, they feel their gift is appreciated when I put it into water and care for it as opposed to throwing it away, so we need to care for the gifts that God has given us.

Consequently, it is possible to have the two-year-old tidying up my shoes and handbag, and the six-year-old tidying the two-year-old's lego. They know just how I like the pillows on the couch, and where to put Daddy's car keys. It doesn't matter whose it is, because we are all working together. I have, at various stages, encouraged the speed of the tidying by offering to put a sweetie in the jars of whichever children are tidying their best, and the jars are given to them at the end of the week, on Friday 'Family Games Night'.

At this point, I would like to say that sorting things into the appropriate places is an incredibly good exercise for their little brains, and you are not doing them any favours if you let them skip this part of the day and do it yourself. Developing pattern-recognition, sorting objects into catagories and planning task-sequencing are all essential building blocks for learning mathematics, as well as reading, time management and many other life skills. Hopefully that is helpful to you not feeling too sorry for them!

Thirdly, let's face it, most of the deep tidying still lies with us, certainly while the children are young, and I suspect when they are older as well! So, once a week, if possible, I find one to two hours to go through the whole house and tackle the deep sorting of things that have been tidied up into the wrong boxes, straightening of the clothes and shoes in the cupboard, unpacking the many handbags and baby bags my girls have collected things into, and throwing out the 'special' items that have been collected over the week, like shrinking balloons, unfinished Sunday-school art, and other such 'treasure'.

That includes looking under the beds and couches, so I am very happy to announce, that on the day my husband rearranged our furniture in front of everyone, I was relieved and grateful to find only a cleanly swept floor!

7 DISCIPLINE

"Give it!" I hear an unnamed child of mine shout at a younger brother, who toddled in to the room and helped himself to the roof of the Lego house that was being built... So, do I get out of my cozy bed and go and address the way he is speaking, or do I pretend I didn't hear? Sadly, I take the third option of yelling through the walls, "Ask nicely and he'll give it back to you!"

On a good discipline day, I have received the compliment of being asked how I discipline my children. (Now I'm smiling, wondering if I could have been mistaken to take the comment as a compliment?) I think when us moms ask another mom that question we're really hoping for a quick fix solution.

They say a stitch in time saves nine. If you don't mend it straight away, it's likely to get worse and take more mending later. 'Sew Simple' - have you heard of it? It's a fabulous fabric glue that you can use for mending torn seams. Unfortunately, there is no such thing in the world of discipline. The thing with disciplining our children is never to let a single thing slide (I know, impossible, just go with me on this one). It is to correct each little behavioral error as it happens (preferably getting out of bed to go and sort it out!). To borrow from our idiom, a 'smack' in time saves nine. It is not fair to ignore the first few offenses and then smack or discipline the next one 'out of the blue'. Our poor children at least need to know that, for example, speaking rudely to one's little brother, is always unacceptable and punished, not only on randomly selected occasions. 'Jackpot' spankings, handed out at a few random moments, are far crueler, and possibly could be considered abusive, as opposed to consistent discipline, even if that means five smacks in half an hour for the same offense. In the latter case, you are far more likely to have the rest of the day pass by incident free. We need to be 'consistent' to be kind.

The Three D's

To help us process how various deviances should be disciplined, we have a guideline in our home. Spankings are only, and always, handed out for three reasons: Disobedience; Dishonouring people; and Disrespecting property. If a child's behaviour is undesirable, but doesn't fall into one of these three categories, then it is dealt with in an alternative way.

Disobedience is the willful disregard to an understood command. Sometimes we make suggestions to our children that they should put on a jersey, or tidy their room. Other times we tell them to. When they know that you are asking them to do something and not just strongly suggesting, then they need to be obedient. Immediately obedient.

I mention suggestions because I think it's great to give our children as much freedom to learn to make wise decisions as they can handle. God certainly allows us to develop our characters and learn wisdom that way. We can't expect to raise leaders and world changers out of sheep.

But there are also times, many times, when obedience is necessary and expected. Sometimes, even, I give my children specific commands just so they can practice their obedience.

"Time to get out of the pool."

"Can we have one more jump, please?"

"Not today."
But mostly I say 'Yes' as often as possible, in imitation of our God of whom the bible says "no good thing does He withhold" from us, His children. (Psalm 84:11). The same source of wisdom also tells us in Proverbs 23:13, "Do not withhold discipline from a child."

As far as obedience goes, there is certainly no room for "I'm counting to three and then you better put that down..." Most often when it comes to obedience, it needs to be immediate for it to be effective. There are countless safety scenarios that require immediate obedience, and plus it is just time-consuming and humiliating to have to have your instructions weighted with a '1, 2, 3' for them to have value.

A whined "Why can't I?" is not a legitimate question, it is a challenge of authority. Legitimate questions are great, and important, and should be given suitable attention and explanation. But a legitimate question comes after the intent to obey the instruction. "Yes, Mom. (Jump up to obey.) Can I ask why we have to do that now?" Knowing and understanding our children will help us to recognise the motivation behind a question, so that we can discipline dissension, and honour the desire to understand reasons.

Willful disobedience in our home does not get a second chance. From when they can talk, our children are taught the phrase, "Yes, Mom." It is a phrase that we practice with our toddlers and preschoolers. "When Mommy asks you to do something, what do you say?" When our two or three-year old says to an instruction to tidy up, "I don't want to..." we tease them saying, "Uh-oh, you forgot your words! What do you say to Mommy/Daddy?" And they smile and remember, "Yes, Mom!"

After that gentle reminder, at most, there is no more room for argument. Disobedience gets a smack every time.

It must be pointed out that the more time you spend with your young children, the more likely you are to correctly discern between innocent distraction and defiant disobedience. I love to take naps with my little boys, and it will take many reminders that it's naptime before they finally fall asleep. We will be lying there quietly and one will begin to sing. When I remind them to be quiet, they obey willingly, but a few moments later will be trying to touch their nose with their toes. Each time I remind them, they quickly go back to trying to fall asleep. Because I have been with them throughout the experience, I know that it is not defiance, so when at bedtime it takes a few reminders after lights out for them to fall asleep, I am happy that a smack is not always necessary. It is really helpful to know your children's capabilities as they grow and develop so that you can discipline with confidence, and not cruelty.

Dishonouring people is an area that I think we underestimate our children's understanding in. Children know from very young what is a nice way to treat people, and what is rude. If you tell your four-year-old to change his tone of voice, or else get a smack for being disrespectful, you'll be amazed at his ability to know the difference between a rude tone and a polite one.
Dishonour of parents, siblings, friends, and even animals, is not an area that requires obedience. We don't need to tell them how to treat people. As they are being rude, they are well aware that their behaviour is unacceptable. For that reason, dishonouring people is worthy of getting a smack in our home.

Similarly, a child who is tearing apart a book, or throwing a toy car against the wall, is well aware that his behaviour is destructive and unacceptable. When caught in the act, he doesn't need to first be given a warning that he must obey. He is expecting to be punished when he looks up and sees that you have seen what he's done, and we shouldn't disappoint him by being soft.
However, a child who has dropped a glass that he was carrying to the kitchen, even if he was being somewhat irresponsible in the way he was doing it, does not need to be smacked or shouted out. As he looks at you in horror, realising what he has done, he needs to be given grace, and a gentle reminder that we have taught him to carry one thing at a time for a reason. He was not trying to be disobedient, and neither was he trying to be disrespectful of

property. He was simply seeing if he could manage to do something in the carefree, capable way he sees grownups doing it.

That reminds me of an important point when disciplining. We need to punish the intent, not the result. Whether the juice is spilled on the grass outside, or on your favourite rug, the lesson is the same. Whether a child naughtily throws a rubber duckie, or your smartphone, the discipline should be equal!

Is Spanking the Christian Way of Discipline?

Spankings have in some circles, and some countries, become taboo, and Christians have been notorious for favouring this method of discipline. The paraphrased bible verse, 'Spare the rod and spoil the child', has been used both to argue for God's approval of spankings, and to point out the alleged abusive discipline of Christian parents who spank their children.

The bible verse actually reads, "He who spares the rod hates his son, but he who loves him is careful to discipline him." (Proverbs 13: 24)

Biblically speaking, I believe God does not prescribe the method of discipline so much as exhort parents not to "withhold discipline" (Proverbs 23:13) from their children. "God disciplines those He loves" (Proverbs 3:12), but history shows us that He disciplines in different ways for different people and at different times.

I don't think spanking is 'God's way' and that we are obliged to discipline our children with it as Christians, but I do think He is okay with loving discipline in this form.

More importantly, God wants us not to neglect our children, but to be actively involved in training them and preparing them for their futures. He exhorts parents to love their children enough to guide them with discipline and to protect them from falling prey to laziness, and unruliness, and all the dangers that come with being untaught and undisciplined.

The bible's references to discipline are incredibly loving and show a heart that is devoted to the best interests of the child. Proverbs 3:12 says, "The Lord disciplines those He loves, as a father the son he delights in." Proverbs 19:18 says, "Discipline your son, for in that there is hope; do not be a willing party to his death."

It speaks of the peace and joy that reigns in a home where discipline is well utilized: Proverbs 29:17 "Discipline your son, and he will give you peace; he will bring delight to your soul." Let your home be a home of harmony and love, where each family member, and even guests, can find a place of rest and tranquility.

Discipline, correctly administered, is not abuse. Lack of discipline, in the name of children's rights or anything else, is neglect. Proverbs 29:15 "The rod of correction imparts wisdom, but a child left to himself disgraces his mother." It is sad to see when a child is discriminated against by his/her teachers and peers and other adults, due to that child's ill-discipline. It is a gift to train and teach our children in how to be respectful, and how to play fair in the real world, where they are not the centre.

Whether it's spanking, time-outs, reality discipline, privileges removed, or any other new idea, discipline must be effective and consistent. Ideally, the child should expect it. There should be no surprise smacks or yells or slaps. It should communicate love and be for training.

All methods of discipline need to be applied with wisdom and discernment. The wrong type of discipline applied to the wrong child or in the wrong way can be harmful to their development. This does not just apply to smacks. To send a child to their room, or to the naughty corner, or even the 'get-good' chair, when that particular child's love language is being together with you, may be crueler than a quick smack. By disciplining with the time-out method you are affectively denying that child love in the way that he understands it.

Spanking is a tool for discipline, that when administered with love, a gentle heart and without anger, can be a tool that is very effective. My children have shown and communicated no fear of me whatsoever, and are quite free to jump into my arms with a stinging bottom. When I have asked if smacks scare them or are nasty, they have replied, "No, just sore." Smacks are unpleasant, and so discipline should be.

Training, Not Taunting

It is important to keep uppermost in our minds when bringing up children that we are in the training phase of life. When a child does something wrong, or stupid, we are not to get angry.

> Your role is to train and teach, to correct and discipline, but not to belittle.

Beware of insulting or mocking your children when they fall short. Watch out for comments from your mouth like, "I can't believe you still spill everywhere at your age," or "What is the matter with you?" or "You are so bad at that."

Your role is to train and teach, to correct and discipline, but not to belittle. Your tone of voice is more potentially destructive than any application of discipline. To use your words to speak down to your children is an abuse of power.

In everything, train with patience and self control: "Remember, my child, I have taught you not to slam doors."; "My girl, you need to try and be more careful when you eat."; "My child, that is not how we treat our pets. That was mean, and we need to give you a smack for that to help you remember not to do that again."

Effective Discipline

If you choose to issue smacks for certain offenses in your home, it is important to give thought beforehand as to where, with what, and how hard you will administer this discipline.

A rule of thumb for us is that discipline needs to effect change. If you tap your child on the hand, or even just give them a frown, and they never want to do that naughty thing again, then that is discipline enough. However, if you have given your child a good solid spanking and he laughs in your face and goes back to doing what he was doing, then you need to keep looking for a more effective discipline!

It is interesting to note that God seems to administer the least amount of discipline that is required for change. Proverbs speaks frequently about a wise person responding to a gentle rebuke. If our children are wise and easily trained, then discipline should be minimal. If they are stubborn then discipline must be stronger, for their own good.

Older babies and young toddlers need to be disciplined on the spot, and usually a smack on the hand or the nappy is sufficient to upset them and cause them to be obedient. Some babies will respond just as well to a stern voice and a frown, and others might require a bit of a stinger for them to take any notice. The important thing is to measure the effect of the discipline – don't waste your time and their sweet bottoms by smacking for no reason. The kind thing is to administer the least discipline that IS EFFECTIVE.

I don't have a very strong stance on where (location-wise) a smack should be given, but I do think that we need to always show our children respect. If they are old enough to be embarrassed or humiliated, then I think it is courteous to take them to a private room. I usually ask them to go to a bedroom and then ask them to take their shorts down themselves and put their hands on the bed. I expect them to respect me enough to do this otherwise they will receive further discipline for disrespect. I really don't want to be chasing my darling children whom I love around the house wielding a wooden spoon and trying to grab them by the arm while they are screaming. It is chaotic and disrespectful on both sides, and would leave a child feeling very unsafe and frightened. They need to know that the situation is under control and that we will continue to respect each other even during discipline.

I am quite comfortable to smack with my hand, because I am doing it in a controlled environment that is definitely defined as a time of discipline. It has been proposed that hands should only be used for loving, but seeing as I am not lunging out to smack my children when they are not expecting it, I have not found that they show any fear or confusion when I reach out to touch them in love. However, I don't really love having a stinging hand, and so when a pat with the hand is no longer effective, I will move on to using a little paddle of sorts for my older toddlers and young children.

Tantrums

Kids. You gotta love them. No really, you've got to. It's a rule.

My nine-year-old relays very long and repetitive stories to me every time she comes home from school, all about the politics of Grade 3 girls. It's hard to believe I was ever that age.

The other day she had a pearler. "Mom, Jemma (not her real name) was at the shops with her mom this weekend, and she wanted something but her mom said, 'No', so she fake-cried and then she got it."

Meaningful pause, while I wonder about the point of this story...

"Mom, will that work for me?"

Much hysterical laughter from me. Less from her.

So - tantrums. What to do about them? Well, I think my daughter has brought up a very good point that every child and toddler is wondering about tantrums: "Will it work for me?"

I guess that is a good starting point. What works in your house? Your child is compiling a mental database as she learns about the world: 'When I ask like this, is it effective?'; 'When I keep asking a hundred times, is that more effective?'; 'When I snatch, does that mean I get what I want?'; 'When I cry, does that work for me?'.

For me, it's a good reason why you want to be with your children when they are young and to be training them on a minute-by-minute basis. If your children are playing unsupervised, and they snatch, chances are, that is more effective than asking nicely. However, if you are watching them, chances are they more often land up successfully acquiring what they want by asking nicely, than by snatching.

Your children need to know that you mean business, that you are a person of your word. They need to know that once you have spoken decisively, you will not change your mind because of emotional outbursts. If you let it go with the little things - allow whining to work sometimes, allow nagging to work sometimes - then when you put your foot down, your kids will just up the whining to a tantrum to get you to change your mind. A child who knows that 'No' means 'No' is far less likely to throw in an extra show if they know they're likely to just get the same result - still a 'No'!

If you are consistent with this in the early years, you might have a handful of tantrums from your toddler, but really, by two and a half, he should have figured out that they don't work.

That being said, what if that ship has already sailed and you now have a tantrum-throwing child? One of my principles of parenting is to treat my children with respect. In this situation, I wouldn't grab a child and remove them from a situation against their will. On the same hand I expect respect from them. My response to a child throwing a tantrum would be to very sternly say, "How you are behaving is unacceptable. Get up, right now, and come with me to your room, and we can talk about what you want." If the child does not obey, I would say, "If I have to pick you up and take you to your room, you will get an extra smack for disobedience. You are already going to get a smack for acting disrespectfully. If you get up and walk to your room now, you will only get one smack, but if I have to take you to your room, you will get two smacks."

I think that this gives the child a little bit of power, in that they are able to make a decision and maintain their dignity, which is important to a child who feels powerless. Also, because you are going with them to their room, to discipline them, yes, but also to help them solve their problem, they will hopefully not feel abandoned to their out-of-control emotions. But really, I think tantrums are best avoided by teaching them in non-stressful times, like chatting around the dinner table, how ineffective a tantrum would be. Tantrums are not just as a result of children not getting what they want, but rather of children not feeling heard or understood. Teach your children how to get their own way, by teaching them how to communicate, how to reason, how to explain why their request is important to them. And listen to your children when they speak. Give them the courtesy of explaining to them the reason for your decisions when you are not giving them what they want. But also teach them that sometimes they need to accept 'No' for an answer without an immediate explanation.

We are not only to discipline our children, but to teach them. Talk to them often, play out different scenarios, just as a coach would play out how to catch different passes. Prepare your children for life, and they will handle it better when the pass is thrown 'in the game'.

A Mommy's Tell

How do your kids know when you're being serious? As in, 'listen to me this instant' kind-of serious? I remember being in a moms' group years ago where one mom was complaining that her young child always laughed when she disciplined her. An older mommy replied, "Well, that's because you haven't found your mommy voice yet." And it was true - this young mommy loved, played and disciplined all in the same manner.

Now personally, I don't want to be raising my voice at my children and sounding like a scary lady every time I want them to listen to me, so I decided to find another 'tell'. Our kids know us intimately, and can read our facial expressions, body language, and voice intonations from when they are babies - they have to - it's essential for their survival! (And their smack avoidance!)

So, I looked in the mirror in the privacy of my own home, and tried on various 'tells':
• Was I going to raise my eyebrows?
• Point my finger?

- Say, "Mommy says..." (A bit like Simon says - when 'Mommy says' you have to do it!)
- Change my tone of voice?
- Add 'now' to my command?

And then I chose a 'tell' that my children would recognise meant, "Do not argue. This is not up for discussion. I want immediate obedience." But, also, that I was happy would be a non-scary, non-attention drawing, non-embarrassing thing that I could easily do in public, or while visiting an old couple in their tiny townhouse full of breakable ornaments.

It has worked for me, so I recommend that you also find a 'mommy tell' that will help your children know when you are not joking or suggesting, but expecting obedience.

Truthful Consistency

My two year old son called me on my inconsistency the other night. I had told him to eat up his supper or he would get a smack for disobedience. (I wouldn't give him a smack for not eating ordinarily - I'm quite ok with them not finishing their supper if they've had enough, and it's not on my list of the 'Three D's'. It was just that this time I had specifically given him a little bit and asked him to finish it, because he was developing a bad habit of being fussy.)

Well, anyhow, I saw that he was yawning and looking exhausted, and I didn't want to force him to do something he was not able to do if he was too tired to try, so I excused him from the table.

"But no, Mummy. You said I must finish or get a smack."

Uh-oh. Now he knew I was being inconsistent and not following through on a promised punishment. I explained to him that I was letting him off because I could see he was tired, and reminded him that we had had a very late night the night before with a year-end function. (I didn't want to give him the idea that he could just claim tiredness every time he didn't want to finish his dinner.) I assured him that tomorrow night he would eat all his dinner, and I made sure to stay true to that word. Interestingly enough, he was quite put out by my unpredictable behaviour and kept asking me why he was excused.

I think it's essential that our children expect truthful consistency from us. I'm glad that he expected follow through from me, even though I duffed it that time. We have to be so careful what we say will happen as potential punishments. Our kids are not silly - of course not - we gave them our cleverness and have suffered with porridge brain ever since!

So when we say that they will get left behind if they don't hurry up - we better have a babysitter lined up! Or that they will get a smack if they misbehave in the shops, we better have a plan for where and how, and follow through if necessary. It is impossible to make your child respond positively to threats that seldom materialise. Even if 50% or 75% of discipline threats are followed through with, your children might be happy with those odds and willing to take the risk in order to keep doing what they want to do instead of listening to you.

When we pull our 'mommy's tell' (our serious face or wagging finger that shows we mean business), our kids should expect truthful consistency from us every time. That way, we actually need to administer a lot less discipline. They know their boundaries and they can predict their parents' behaviour - such a comforting thing for a child!

We need to give our kids the security of knowing they should believe us when we talk, and that they can trust us to be the same yesterday, today and tomorrow. It requires us thinking carefully before we speak in anger or irritation, and it requires us understanding that consistency is love - often a better kind of love, a more long-lasting, security-bringing kind of love, than giving in to those cute little faces and excuses.

Bribery vs. Reward

We've heard that bribery is not a good way of getting desired behaviour out of our children, but what exactly constitutes bribery, and are there reasonable reasons for offering rewards to our children?

If a spanking is the consequence of disobedience, then to tell our child that if they listen, they'll get a sweet, is definitely counter-productive. They must listen because the person speaking has the God-given authority to teach, train and protect them, and that is reason enough!

However, when our child is trying to learn a new skill, or would benefit from extra motivation, then a reward is a great idea. A toddler who is nervous or unsure about using the toilet is not being disobedient to refuse to do so. It is just outside of their perceived ability and no amount of threats or fear will motivate them to do so. However, a promise of a reward might well be all they need to give the new challenge a try. For me, sweeties are an essential part of potty training! However, once going to the toilet is within the realm of their capability, then they need to do so for the sake of obedience. At that point, when they are confused as to why a 'No. 2' no longer comes with a jelly tot, you can explain that they are so clever, they already know how to use the toilet - now they will get a sweetie as a prize when they learn to ride their bike.

Our children look forward to being allowed to go to the shops and choose a 'grownup' chocolate (a slab) to share with the family when they swim their first length of the swimming pool. (They share it because sharing is the done thing, because a whole slab of chocolate is a bit much for them, and because it gets their siblings cheering for them to swim a length!)

Our holiday in the mountains was offered as a reward for an outstanding term's work form our school children - and they definitely deserved it and were motivated to keep up their best in the last week or two as they were getting tired.

Self-discipline

The purpose of discipline is not to control or to create a dependency of our children on us. We want them to learn what is good for them, and good for achieving their purpose in this world, and to learn how to apply those things themselves. As Paul says in 1 Corinthians 9:26-27, "I do not run like a man running aimlessly; I do not fight like a man beating the air. No, I beat my body and make it my slave so that after I have preached to others, I myself will not be disqualified for the prize."

Each year, particularly as our children reach school-going age, they need to learn how to discipline themselves. This should be broken down to their level. I joke with my older kids, saying, "Self! That is not allowed! Come on, Self!"

It is helpful to our children when we communicate with them about our weaknesses and mistakes and explain to them how we have learned to overcome some of them. Recently, I commiserated with my children how I had failed to follow the advice of someone who was more knowledgeable than me in a certain area. It had had nearly disastrous consequences for me and I told them how I had learned how important it was to listen to wise people's advice.

When I am exercising self-discipline I do it out loud. "That wasn't a kind thing to do, Jacs. Let's try that again." Bring what seems like adult perfection into reach for them. Remember, though, when exercising self-discipline to speak respectfully to yourself. When my children criticise themselves, I am quick to tell them to speak nicely to my precious little boy or girl. Self-discipline needs to be constructive.

It is great to motivate our children away from needing discipline by explaining to them that as soon as they know what is expected of them in a certain area and are able to discipline themselves to stick to those expectations then they no longer need us to discipline them about that anymore. Our little boy knew that when he had learned what it meant to be a Mun-Gavin boy and was fairly consistent in being respectful of people and property even when he didn't know we were watching, then he was old enough to go to school, because we trusted him to obey his teacher and respect his friends on his own.

Similarly, when our school children are old enough to know what movies they are allowed to watch or what activities they are allowed to get up to, then they will be awarded the freedom of going to play at a friend's house.

When they are able to do their homework without being asked, then we will hand over the discipline in that area to them. They are excited and motivated to apply self-discipline because it has fantastic consequences for their freedom! Until then, they understand that they submit to our discipline for their protection and good.

Follow Through

In parenting, most people know that they should be consistent with their discipline, that they should spend time with their kids, that they should lead by example... it's just the follow through, or lack of follow through, that makes the difference between averagely good parents and great parents.

Similarly, in marriage most men know they should prioritise their families, that they should tell their wives they're beautiful, that they should play cricket with their boys and be home for dinner... Just as most wives know they shouldn't hold their bodies back from their husbands, that they should look attractive when he walks through the door, that they shouldn't nag and whine...

But man, the follow through makes all the difference. Most of us don't even have willpower over what we eat, let alone anything else! We need to be a little more like athletes - able to beat ourselves into submission and choose our behaviour - instead of being tossed about by our whims and desires.

Yes, we may be young moms in a physically demanding stage of our lives. Yes, we may be facing challenges and life may be a little overwhelming. But let's get a hold of ourselves! Let's get life into perspective. I mean, we can sleep when we're dead!

Life is short, and we're not just fighting for flat stomachs here. This is not just 'diet willpower'. We're fighting for our marriages, for our children to turn out right, for God's reputation in the world as people look at us Christians, for His kingdom to be established, for a war to be won. My marriage and my children will NOT be casualties, simply because I didn't have the strength to follow through on what I knew I needed to do. More than that - they will be assets and shining examples of what we can achieve with a little more determination and a little more commitment to saying 'Yes' to the right things.

8 DEVELOPING GODLY CHARACTER

I know we're all born desperately wicked by nature, and our inclination is towards selfishness and self-preservation (well, maybe not you, but definitely the people in our family!), but don't you just love it when something of God's goodness is reflected - from God, sometimes via us, and then into our children - and they come up with the most thoughtful, beautiful ideas?

We had such an experience recently when there were floods happening across the country. Around the dinner table at night we try to engage our children in conversations, and on this particular night we were talking about the weather, and the news that had spoken of people losing their homes. My four year old son was very concerned about people being outside in the rain at night, with their homes having been washed away. For weeks, he watched out the windows when we drove on the freeway and noted the feeble structures that some people lived under and worried about whether or not they would withstand the next rainfall.

A few weeks later, I decided to take my kids to a toyshop because they all had birthday money from the previous few months and I thought it would be exciting to let them choose something they wanted. We walked around the shop for close on an hour and each one of them decided that, though there were lots of things they would enjoy owning, there was nothing that they really needed. After an hour of having a hungry 10kg baby strapped to my chest and keeping track of four children running around, we left the shop with the heaviness of an exhausting and unsuccessful shopping expedition. Of course, we went straight to the shopping centre toilets to make all our wee's before heading to the car and, while crowding the six of us into the family cubicle, we had our 'God-reflection' moment.

I am not sure whose idea it was because it seemed to come to all of them at once, but my children decided that instead of wasting their money on toys they didn't need, they were going to put all their money together, and start saving to help the people who didn't have homes. The idea progressed, and after sneakily questioning our housekeeper and finding out that her home is made of mud and straw and struggles to withstand the weather, they have decided to save their birthday and Christmas money for the next few years so that they can build a brick house for her and her family. They have even gone so far as to ask their grandparents and aunt/uncles to rather give them money than presents, if they want to spoil them for birthdays/Christmas, so that it can go into the fund.

Many times our children will display beautiful reflections of God's character, and when you as parents are doing the same thing, thanks to God's gracious work in you, you will up the frequency of this happening. Still, we want to develop our children's Godly characters, and there are definitely things we can do to help this along.

Privileged or Spoiled?

In the last sentence of the above story I specified, "if they want to spoil them". When something happens regularly, we come to expect it, which is generally what makes us spoiled. I am quite clear with my children about what their rights are, and what is a privilege beyond what they have a right to.

So for example, a birthday gift is a privilege. The fact that they have been privileged enough to get one every birthday so far, does not make it an expected right. (Do you know, when we gave our housekeeper a birthday gift, it was the first birthday gift she had ever received?) On the night before their birthdays, we ask excitedly, "Do you think you might even get a present tomorrow? That would be special! But even if you don't, we'll all still give you a hug and say 'Happy birthday' to you. Exciting, hey?"

Birthday parties are a privilege. "Mommy and Daddy have been talking, and we've decided that we would like to give you a party for your birthday this year. Would you like that?"

Water is a right. Juice is a privilege. If they are ever at someone else's house or are invited out to a restaurant by another family, or even with us, I prefer for them to ask only for water until they are offered something more. Of course, our two-year-old sits down in a restaurant and says, "Where my milkshake?". Guess he's still learning that one.

Sweets are a privilege. Especially while we're grocery shopping! God allows us to ask Him for special treats, and so our children are allowed to ask us, too, but never with an expectation that it is their right. When I do give them sweets, or even just a cup of juice at home, they giggle in delight, and say, "Mom! Why are you spoiling us?".

Education is a privilege. Isn't it? It's an incredible privilege. Help them to understand that. There should be no griping about homework. You want your own car one day? You want to have tons of money to buy sweets or build houses for people? Then say, "Thank you so much, Daddy, for working hard so we can go to school," and, "Thank you, teacher, for all your hard work in preparing a lesson for us." Your children imitate you. It's a fact that most children will only ever become as educated as their mothers are. Your father might have a phD, but if your mom doesn't have her Matric, you're unlikely to get yours. Mothers either instill a love for learning in their children... or they don't.

A warm bed and a dry shelter is a privilege. A loving family is a privilege. A car is a privilege. Give thanks in all things, and give your children the joy of being extremely privileged, without being spoiled.

Biblical Standards

The bible is an essential tool in teaching all things to our children. Whether you are teaching them to love one another and treat each other with respect or to share or to be kind or to be honest, there are scriptures to reinforce the lessons, or better yet, to *set* the lessons. We have all been taught to "do to others what you would have them do to you." (Luke 6:31). Even more than that, we need to follow Jesus' teaching to "Love one another as [he has] loved [us]", giving up our lives for one another. (John 15:12-13).

Reading the bible to our children and familiarising them with Jesus' teachings will go a long way to molding their characters. They will have their own reference to which they can measure their behaviour.

It also helps us in knowing what standard we should set. You and your spouse will most probably have been brought up with slightly different rules and priorities in your homes. When we are familiar with the standards God has for us and the lessons in the bible, then we are able to apply them to daily scenarios in our lives and our parenting.

Low Expectations, High Demand

One of the most helpful lessons I have ever had in parenting has come out of time spent with God. Not surprisingly, He is an incredible source of wisdom! After all, we are doing this for Him, so it's in His best interest to help us. He has promised in 2 Corinthians 9:8 that He "is able to make all grace abound to you, so that in all things at all times, having all that you need, you will abound in every good work". He equips us for this parenting job that He has given us.

In my time with Him, God showed me that by His standards, anything less than perfection is sin. He asks of us , His children, that we would "be perfect, therefore as [our] heavenly Father is perfect." (Matthew 5:48). Of course, He knows we can't actually attain perfection, which is why He accredits it to us by His grace. Hebrews 10:14 says that "by one sacrifice [His death] He has made perfect forever those who are being made holy." It goes on to say in verse 17, "Their sins and lawless acts I will remember no more."

If we are parenting in imitation of God, what should our standard be for our children? Perfection! We ask for perfection, and anything less is not good enough. But, and this is the clever part, we *expect* nothing. The bible says about God, "As a father has compassion on his children, so the Lord has compassion on those who fear Him; for He knows how we are formed, He remembers that we are dust." (Psalm 104:13-14). In another translation it says He remembers we are "but mud".

If we expect our children to fall short of perfect obedience, then it doesn't rock our world or disappoint us when they do. You are far less likely to lose your temper with your child when you are not surprised at their behaviour. When your child throws your cellphone in the toilet for the fourth time, you will have the power to calmly and lovingly say, "No, my love, I've told you not to do that. We're going to have to give you a smack so you can remember to listen to what I say."

Focus on Giving

My kids are models to me of generosity - I have a lot to learn from them. In our home in the weeks before Christmas, because I am trying to think about what to buy our very large extended family for Christmas, our focus is on giving, as opposed to receiving, presents. I seldom, if ever, ask my kids what they want for Christmas. Sometimes a granny or aunty might particularly want me to ask, but mostly our conversation about Christmas presents is around what we want to get for others. The children love this and are totally on-board. They are so happy to cut costs on grocery bills and any other area in order to save to buy presents. They prefer to eat porridge rather than cereal in the morning, and phutu and beans as opposed to chicken 'a la king' for dinner. They are careful to turn off taps when they wash their hands, and if it's still dripping they come and ask us to turn it off for them. All of this is because they are aware that money is finite, but they want to be generous with our extended families for Christmas. (This from the two-year-old to the nine-year-old.)

Because they have also helped in thinking about what to buy each person and if not in the shopping itself then definitely in the wrapping, their attention has become focused on wanting to watch the others open their gifts on the day as much as, if not more than, on opening their own gifts.

It's a small adjustment, and to be honest, I don't even think it has been that intentional… but it certainly is pleasant to enjoy giving gifts as a family as opposed to having children spoiled and whining about what they want to get.

We often refer to the lesson in Luke 3:11 which says, "The man with two tunics should share with him who has none." As often as we have opportunity, which is pretty often, we go through our toys and clothes and give away duplicates. When my girls heard of a child their age who had no shoes, they found that they had two pairs of gumboots, two pairs of sandles, and two pairs of takkies, so they gave away one of each. We don't need two rain jackets, or more than a couple of dresses. One doll each is sufficient. We keep our wardrobes to a minimum, and rather store up treasures in heaven where moth and rust do not destroy. There is no escaping the fact that children reason on a practical level and if we want them to learn biblical lessons then we are going to have to act them out. They won't let you get away with having multiple pairs of shoes to wear with the same type of outfit in your cupboard either!

What You Celebrate, You Generate

A guest in our home kindly brought along some little packets of sweets and gave one to each of my children. They refused to eat them all, INSISTING that they each give one or two to Dad, and Mom, offer to our guest, and then share with each other. This is very normal amongst these unusual children of mine. This was not a staged incident!

Arguments have been known to break out, that go, "You have the last apple."

"No, you can."

"No, please will you?"

And it's not because they don't like apples!

It's because sharing is celebrated. Sharing is cool. And sharing is also trained. Our children don't really have their own toys. Of course, they are allowed to keep special things away from younger brothers who might break them. But in general, everything is shared.

When you celebrate kindness, your children will be motivated to keep being kind, or to imitate their sibling who received the praise for it. When you celebrate hard work, they will do what it takes to be acknowledged by you in this area. As we all know, children need attention, and they will pick up whether it's quicker and easier to get negative attention or positive attention.

Start from when they are babies. When our one-year-old is told, "Don't touch that," and he listens, he gets actual applause and a "Well done, Kade! You listened to Mommy!" Don't do a song and a dance because they're not eating. Do a song and a dance when they do eat!

Remember, what you celebrate, you generate.

Life's Not Fair

Children are always complaining that 'life's not fair'. And it seems that grownups are always doing their best to try and make it so life is fair. But the truth is it's not.

It's not fair that some people can have children and some people can't. It's not fair that some children go to sleep at night hungry while their mother's are boiling plain water on the stove to try and placate their children into thinking that dinner will eventually arrive. It's not fair that some people don't have use of their legs, and some children are unable to play and climb and run. It's unfair that children go to sleep at night without blankets, or even roofs. It's unfair that they have to walk miles in rain or heat to get to a school where they don't even have a pencil. No, life is not fair, and I take every opportunity to point out to my children when I see life being unfair for people. But we are not on the 'unfair' side of fair. We are, in most circumstances, on the privileged side of fair.

If ever my children forget, and say, "Why does Jed have the last apple? That's not fair!", I say, "Nope. It's not fair. It's not trying to be fair. It's not fair that your classmate had a birthday and so you got cupcakes at school today, and we didn't. It's not fair that Rourke is still little so he came to the shops with me this morning and we had ice creams. It's not fair. But we each get different privileges at different times."

We just need to help our children to gain perspective of how different people are given privileges and treats at different times, and it is not a lesson that they are unwilling to learn. Don't spoil your children by giving them presents on each others' birthdays, or making sure they all get the same treats at once.

God definitely does NOT treat us all equally. That is obvious by the economic range in our churches. And yet He gives each of us everything we need for life and Godliness. We are never in want, so long as we are looking at what He has given us, and what He thinks is good for us, rather than at what He has given our neighbour. He is not 'fair' but He is always just, always kind, always generous, and always wise.

When our children lose the expectations of fairness, a wonderful thing happens. They are able to be happy for other people and be thankful with others for their joys.

As I was writing this, my three older kids were out riding their bikes and because the fourth one is too little to keep up, Daddy had put him on his back and taken him for a ride on his big bike so he can join in. The others would LOVE to go on Daddy's back, but they're a bit big. So instead of saying, "That's not fair!" I heard them say, "That's so cool, Rourke! Enjoy your ride!". The day before, our eldest was allowed to go to the hotel to join in a 'Tweens Quiz' for 9-12 year olds. The others said, "That's such fun for you, Jada. I hope we come here when I'm nine so I can do that!"

No, life's not fair. But it's more fair for us, so let's be grateful!

9 TEACHING OUR CHILDREN ABOUT AN INVISIBLE GOD

We have a man who works for us in the garden every now and again, called Michael. Michael has helped us do quite a few minor building changes around the property, like fixing a broken part of our wall, knocking through a doorway, painting, and other such projects that the boys just love to be a part of. My two boys just follow Michael around everywhere when he is working, asking for turns to push the wheelbarrow, 'helping' to varnish the jungle gym, mixing cement for him, and basically just slowing him down.

One day, I took all my children to one of the local beaches that they had not been to before. It is quite a spectacular beach, with tall overhanging cliffs giving shade on the sand, and huge boulders everywhere. My almost two year old boy looked around at all of this magnificence, and said in awe, "Wow! Michael made it!".

We collapsed in laughter and tried to explain to him that God had, in fact, made it. He looked around a bit confused, and said, "Oh... God made it."

Clearly I had been unsuccessful in teaching him about God so far! A few months later I caught him staring blankly out the window in a trance. I asked him what he was doing, and he replied matter-of-factly, "Just staring ata trees." Trying to improve on my previous failure, I told him, "Do you know that God made those trees, my boy?"

"Oh... A big God? On a ladder?"

So sweet! I explained to him, of course, that God was very big and He could reach the trees without a ladder, all the while feeling that I was really improving as a 'Sunday School' teacher. That was, until a few days later, when I was telling some friends proudly of the 'big God on a ladder' story, and my little boy pipes up, "God doesn't need a ladder. And also not monkeys. Only me, cause I'm little."

Oh dear! It is a delightful challenge to teach our children about the mysterious things of God, and one full of humour. I'm not sure that I'm qualified to be writing on this subject, because the other day, around the dinner table, while talking about whether or not the Holy Spirit visited our church, my four year old son said, "But that's silly, because you are the Holy Spirit, hey, Dad?" Uh...No. Back to the drawing board, again!

My favourite way of explaining God to young children, is explaining that we have skin on, so we have to stay inside our skin, but God doesn't have skin, so He's allowed to spread out all over the place. We can't see Him, but He's here, and there, and everywhere.

I think our role as parents is two-fold. Teach them to love and worship God, by your example, and teach them to love God's Word, also, I'm afraid, by your example. There are not really any shortcuts.

For the first one, we need to be talking about God all the time, thanking Him aloud throughout the day, expressing love for Him when we have a prayer answered or see something beautiful or just feel love for Him. It is not uncommon to hear in our home, "God is so kind, don't you think? I'm so grateful He put us all together in this family, because I love being with you." Or, "I love God. He is so clever to make these flowers!"

Our children need to see us worshipping God. When my children were being home-schooled, the first thing we did everyday, after our breakfast and getting ready for the day, was stick on some music and sing praises to God. We would sing, and shake or bang on instruments, and I would dance with them, but I would also just get lost in worship while they watched. It was sometimes uncomfortable as I was aware of them staring at me but they have learnt that their parents truly, personally, worship God. I reaped a precious reward one Sunday when my incredibly shy six year old daughter started dancing during worship in church, and then took my hand and pulled me to dance with her. What an amazing moment!

For our second role as parents, teaching them to love His Word, I think our children need to see that we prioritise reading and memorising God's word. It is good for them to sometimes be told, "Not right now, my love. Mommy is just reading about God. Why don't you get your bible and come look at the pictures next to Mommy?" They love imitating you. If you tell them a verse you are trying to remember at the moment, you can bet they will decide memorising is cool and fun.

Teaching our kids about God is a big topic, but, to put it in a sentence: Love God yourself, out loud, and visibly, and you will be giving your children a wonderful gift.

Lest They Forget God

God reminds us countless times to keep retelling our children, and our children's children, about the great things He has done. Good gracious, if you don't write down today the prayers you have prayed so that you can see tomorrow that He has answered them, even those things will go unappreciated.

We are unbelievably forgetful. If you are sensible enough to keep a record of the prayers you have prayed just pick up any of your prayer journals from years gone by to see how God is alive and miraculously working in our lives.

For the sake of our children, and our grandchildren, and for the sake of our God who is never far from us, let us vow to tell of the things He has done this week, last year, in our parents' lives, and in generations gone by.

> Psalm 78: 1-7 (ESV)
> *Listen, my people, to my teaching,*
> *and pay attention to what I say.*
> *I am going to use wise sayings*
> *and explain mysteries from the past,*
> *things we have heard and known,*
> *things that our ancestors told us.*
> *We will not keep them from our children;*
> *we will tell the next generation*
> *about the Lord's power and his great deeds*
> *and the wonderful things he has done.*
> *He gave laws to the people of Israel*
> *and commandments to the descendants of Jacob.*
> *He instructed our ancestors*
> *to teach his laws to their children,*
> *so that the next generation might learn them*
> *and in turn should tell their children.*
> *In this way they also would put their trust in God*
> *and not forget what he has done,*
> *but always obey his commandments.*

To hear God tell it, the most important thing we can teach our children, is to teach them about Him. Teach them the bible stories, teach them the things he has done throughout history and until today.

Bible Reading

There are many beautiful books for children, and it is incredibly beneficial to read OFTEN to your children. They love it, it strengthens your bonds as they cuddle close to see the pictures, it teaches them to share if they have to take turns with their siblings to sit in the prime spot. It is essential for language development, which is essential for question answering and comprehension in their schooling.

But with all these beautiful books available, let us never neglect the reading of the bible to our children. Read the picture book version, read the story book version, read the Good News version, read the NIV. Read one kiddies' bible right through, and then start on another one.

Evening reading before bed is a wonderful routine, and generally results in children that are attentive, because they don't want to be sent to bed without the story! My husband and I find reading in our room quite effective because then if anyone is playing the fool they can be excused to go to their own bed early. This is particularly helpful when the version we are currently reading is a little above the younger children's understanding. It is still good discipline for them to sit and listen, and we make sure to include them as much as possible. Before long we'll be onto a version that is more their level so they're not missing out.

They love it when we ask each of them a question or two about the previous evenings reading before we begin, and that also gives their concentration an extra edge. I'm sure many of you pray with your children before bed, and we have found that when bedtime prayers follow bible reading, they are far more meaningful and directed at God with far more understanding. We find them thanking God for something they've read about or expressing sympathy at a difficulty that God has had to deal with. The relationship is somewhat less about them and somewhat more about the God they are beginning to know more about.

My children's all-time favourite type of bible teaching is when my husband or I have read the story in our own time to brush up on the juicy details only available in the adult versions, and then tell it in our own words, with all the drama and excitement of a campfire story. Some of their favourites are about David's escapades and Paul's adventures.

I will add in one example of our stories, to show you what I mean:

Based on Acts 27:27 - 28:10

Paul was in trouble 'cos he was telling people about Jesus and he wouldn't stop even when he was told to. So Paul was in handcuffs, and some soldiers were taking him on a ship to go to prison somewhere far away. While they were on the ship a big storm came and it was very scary. The rain was pouring down and the thunder was making a big noise and the lightning was flashing BRIGHT and then dark. The wind was blowing and making huge big waves that were making the boat rock so hard that it was nearly tipping over! The sailors who were in charge of the boat were scared that the strong waves bashing the boat were going to break it into pieces. They tied the boat together with ropes to try and stop it from breaking. The big storm carried on the next day, and the next day, and the sailors were so busy being scared that they didn't even eat. But Paul wasn't scared. Even though he was falling from side to side as the boat rocked, and even though it was dark and stormy, with flashing lightning and loud thunder, he was feeling fine. Do you know why?

'Cos God had sent an angel to see him and tell him that God was not going to let him drown in the sea. The angel stood next to Paul, and said, "Don't worry Paul. You are going to get there safely. God will look after you. And also, because God is so kind, He will even save every one of the other people on the ship with you!"

So Paul went to the other guys who were so scared and he said to them, "You don't need to be scared, guys, because God has said we are going to be fine and no one is going to drown. And I know God - he never lies, so you can trust Him." But I don't think those sailors really knew God 'cos they were still scared. After a few days they saw an island and decided to sail for the island so they might be safe there until the storms were finished. They were busy sailing for the island when their ship crashed into a sand bank that was under the water. The ship was stuck on the sand and got smashed to pieces by the waves. All the people had to jump off and swim the rest of the way to the island.

When they got there, they met some people who lived on the island, and luckily those people were very kind to them. Paul and the sailors were cold and wet from swimming, so the people on the island were kind enough to build a fire for them out of wood. Paul also helped to collect some sticks for the fire.

He was busy throwing his stick onto the fire when do you know what happened? You won't believe it... A snake that was hiding IN the piece of wood came out and bit Paul on his finger! He had the snake hanging on his finger, and he YELPED, and shook the snake off into the fire! The island people couldn't believe it! They thought Paul must be a bad guy, because even though he had escaped out of the storm, God had still let him be bitten by a snake! But was Paul a bad guy? The island people watched Paul to see if he was going to start swelling up from the snakebite, or maybe he was going to fall down and die! Do you know what happened to Paul?

Nothing! Absolutely nothing! He didn't even cry, he didn't die, his finger wasn't even sore! God made it all better! So then the island people changed their minds and decided that maybe Paul was a good guy and was friends with God.

They invited Paul to stay in the most important guy's house, which was a big fancy house with a huge big garden. While Paul was there, he found out that the guy whose house he was staying in had a sick dad, so he went to pray for the guy's dad and God healed him. After that all the sick people on the whole island came to see Paul and asked him to talk to God about them and ask God to heal them, and God healed every one of them! So all those people on the island heard about the real God who is strong enough to heal people. And when all the storms were finished then finally Paul and all the sailors could sail on to where they were going.

Our kids just love the way we are able to look them in the eye when we are telling the stories rather than reading them out of a book and it seems to keep the whole range of ages interested because we are looking in their eyes and addressing each one with age-appropriate sentences.

PART III

SPECIFIC PARENTING

10 ROCK-A-BYE WORLD

I'm due to have my fifth baby any day now. I've finally figured out that no one has all the answers. Babies are unique, and caring for them is not an exact science. I am not attempting here to define a workable minute-by-minute routine. This chapter is included to encourage you if you're a new parent, and just to lay some groundwork in your methods of parenting which should make the following years a little easier.

To start out with, parenting was a lot tougher than I thought it would be. I remember struggling through those night feeds, too exhausted to even function properly. I realise that there are a lot of people out there who adapt really easily to their first baby, have them sleeping through by four weeks, and really can't understand what all the fuss is about. While the rest of us are very happy for you, we just ask that you don't judge us but take our word for it that accumulated lack of sleep makes, well, life in general very much more difficult.

For those of you that can identify and would like to have a coffee date so I can tell you a few stories that will make you feel better, pull up a mug.

New parents often ask me, "Why don't people talk about all the difficulties that come with having a baby? No one told us it was going to take us to the edge of ourselves and beyond. No one told us the strain it would put on our marriage." I think the thing is, we know it's hard having a newborn, but it all passes so quickly, and when people think back to it they remember it with fondness. You will, too, although not for the reasons you'd like to imagine. Only in hindsight will you appreciate how often they napped in the day, and how they stayed put in one place, and needed only milk for food! Also, you'll miss their gorgeous smell, and how clean their hands and feet were, and how light they were to carry around.

Second time around, when you have a noisy, dirty toddler demanding your attention for many, many hours in a row, you'll look at your newborn baby and wonder why you found having just one so difficult first time around!

I remember my mom saying to me that when she had her third baby she so enjoyed feeding her at night because it was such a peaceful, special bonding time. I'm pretty sure she was trying to help me see the joy in it, but all I could think was, "What? You're kidding me! You're telling me that my life as a mom is going to be SO difficult, that this painfully exhausting job, that is just about killing me right now, will become the best part of my day?!" Now, looking back, I smile, because she was right. It has become a joy.

I often encourage new moms and dads by saying, "I assure you, you never have to have your first baby again!" And it's true. No baby (excluding exceptional circumstances) will ever be as difficult as your first baby. I'm not 100% sure why that is. I suppose you must get a little better at it - certainly, you know how to read their signals a bit better. And there is also the fact that you spend a LOT less time worrying, which is another factor making it easier. Us first-time moms spend a lot of time worrying when we actually could be sleeping, straining our ears to hear if the baby is making any sounds, and sometimes even getting up to make sure they are breathing.

But I think the overwhelming reason why you'll never find another newborn baby as difficult as the first one, is that your capacity to cope increases. Each new parenting season is a period of stretching, and then settling into your new 'bigness', and it takes a while each time for your capacity-to-cope to catch up with the added responsibilities and expectations on you.

I remember lying in bed one night when my first baby was a few weeks old. I could hear her crying and so I started to feed her. In my dazed state, I heard that she was crying on and off and I was wondering why she was fussing when I was busy feeding her? Why was she being so difficult? She finally settled down, and then about twenty minutes later she started to really scream. I thought, "What now? What is her problem tonight?" Her screaming woke me into a slightly higher state of consciousness than I had been earlier, and as I got up to go to her again, I realised to my horror that the pillow I had been cuddling in my sleep was drenched through. Smelling it confirmed my fear - I had not in fact fed Kiara at all, but had happily fed the pillow all the while that she was moaning! Now she was hysterical and I had no milk left to give her!

On another occasion (not just one other occasion, if I'm honest), I awoke because she was late for a feed and my breasts were feeling too full of milk. I remember lying there and wondering if I should get up and check if she was ok - you know, still breathing and all that. Well, don't judge me if you haven't been there, but I stayed in bed thinking, "I have two options - either she's absolutely fine and if I get up it would just be a silly waste of sleep, or else she's dead, in which case I would handle that news a lot better after another few hours sleep. Either way, it makes more sense to sink back into sleep than to get up and check on her!"

Many new parents feel a lot better after I confess to that story, so I'm gathering it's pretty low! But hey, that's how tired I was, and I know sharing it will help some of you feel less like terrible parents for not coping well with your lack of sleep, either.

A couple with their first baby asked a couple with older kids when they could expect their baby to sleep through the night. The older couple replied, "They start sleeping really well around the same time that they could actually be useful around the house!"

I think your first step as a mom is to embrace and accept the fact that you are in a season of very little sleep. You will become more used to it, and it will eventually improve. A friend of mine went to the doctor to have blood tests and thyroid tests done to figure out why she was so tired all the time. She was sent home with a clean bill of health and the answer that it was because she was a mom!

Good Sleep Habits

I have been asked, "Do you believe in sleep training? Is it effective, and does it fit into God's way of parenting?"

When I have left my older babies to cry at night, I inevitably come through to find their little leg stuck through the cot bars, or their little heads wrapped up in their blankets, or have found them lying in poop up to their ears. Once I found my baby had tried to climb out of his cot and was balancing on the top of his cot side, unable to climb down either way! I conclude that, usually, when a baby cries, they need something. And even if you can't figure out what they need, I think it is still your job to try. Babies need things, and they can't do it for themselves. They need to be burped, they need to be comforted, they need to be fed or given water, they need to be rescued from strange and dangerous situations. And yes, I think God gave them parents so that we could do that for them.

However, on occasion, I have helped my baby in every way I know how and every time I get into bed, just after I get comfortable, they start crying again. Sometimes I just can't get up. I'm sure you can identify. So yes, on those occasions I lie and listen to them cry for a while and find that very often they settle themselves.

I think two things are key to allowing this 'self-soothing' to happen:

Firstly, your baby must be trained to go to sleep on it's own during the day.

It makes sense to start the training with the daytime naps, particularly if you have already gotten into a bad routine at night. To teach your baby to go to sleep without your assistance, you need to catch him when he first shows signs of tiredness - rubbing the eyes, moaning before crying, hiccupping, wanting to be up all the time. At this point you can put your baby into his cot and very often he will be very grateful to fall asleep. It usually works well if you lie him on his tummy because he feels safe with his cheek up against the mattress, but if he prefers his back, put a blanket or cloth up against his cheek.

If your baby is not sighing in relief and sinking into a deep sleep at this stage, try, in this order:

1. Walk out and leave him for one or two minutes, or longer if he is just gently moaning.
2. Try to settle him in his cot without picking him up, by patting his bottom or rubbing his back, and quietly singing/humming a familiar lullaby to him.
3. If he is crying hysterically and showing no signs of wanting to settle, then try moving him into his pram (strapped in so he can't sit up if he is strong enough to do so) and rocking him or pushing him to sleep.
4. As a last resort, pick him up and rock him in your arms. (Ideally, this should not include breastfeeding. Milk should rather be offered at the end of a nap, before play time, and be associated with sustenance, not comfort.)

In this last case, as soon as your baby stops crying and calms down, I would go back to Step 1 of putting him down, still awake, and trying to settle him in his cot. We are aiming to get him to understand that his cot (or his pram) is the place to sleep, not Mommy's chest! Even if you have to settle his hysterics by picking him up five times before getting him to fall asleep, we want him to finally give in to sleep when he's lying in his cot. Even stubborn children will finally figure out that to sleep, he needs to be in his cot. Mom is not going to hold him for his whole nap, or until he is in a deep sleep.

If you persevere with this for a week or so during the day, you should finally get him to fall asleep in his cot without fussing. And that means he can also fall asleep in his cot on his own when he wakes up in the middle of the night after each REM cycle!

The second key to self-soothing is giving your baby a few minutes, both during the day and the night, to have the chance to calm himself before rushing to pick him up.

A baby who is given attention at every peep, becomes a very demanding and dependent baby. On the other hand, a baby who is left to cry for hours at night as done with some extreme sleep training methods, is going to be insecure and needy. We need to find a balance. A moaning baby can be left for a while, but a hysterical baby seldom, if ever, calms itself without your help.

But I must say that the balance is not on the side of you returning in a hurry to getting ten hours of beauty sleep. It's not easy, and if you're a new mom, I assure you that you do adjust and become used to it. My prayer is that, seeing as we are going to be in heaven for eternity, God wouldn't mind if we took the first hundred years just to sleep!

Reading Signals

Life with your baby will be a whole lot simpler if you understand each other. I think the best way to understand your baby is to spend time watching them and knowing them. Even though I have had a couple of babies, I still think a first-time mom is more likely to understand her *own* baby than I am likely to understand her baby.

However, if you are clueless as to what sleeping and eating patterns to expect from your baby at each age, then you will struggle to understand his signals. You need to be watching him closely for his signs that he needs something, plus you need to have a clue as to what he might be asking for.

A sign that your baby might be needing something is that he is dissatisfied – he is moaning and pulling disgruntled faces. When you try to distract him he is not very interested and you can't hold his attention as long as you were able to a few minutes earlier. He might start to hiccup, indicating that he is over-stimulated or tired. If he is older and is crawling or walking, you might find that he just wants to be up, and every time you put him down, even with a favourite toy, he starts to cry.

The trick is to catch the signals early. You don't want to leave him to be miserable for half an hour, or to keep distracting him until he is completely overtired. By that stage it will be very difficult to get him to sleep. An overtired baby will often become completely hysterical when you try and put him down to sleep and you might have missed your chance altogether. Then he will just be miserable for hours, until he is completely exhausted.

On the other hand, if you are unaware of his expected needs during the day, you might think he is playing up because he is tired, when all he wants is a drink of water. Then, when you put him into his cot, he will scream in frustration because you have misunderstood him and he fears you may never 'get it' that he is just thirsty or hungry!

Baby Routine

Of course a baby's routine will be varying almost every month as he grows, and I found it incredibly helpful with my first baby to go to a well-baby clinic at least monthly to get advice. Failing that, it might be good to have a good baby book that you trust.

The important thing is to *have* a routine, preferably from someone who knows what they're talking about, like a current-day mom who has happy, healthy children, or a nurse who specialises in young babies. The routine should at least include what meals to feed the baby as well as what nap-times to expect from him.

A baby who is in a routine is likely to be a lot more settled and happy as his body becomes used to knowing when it will be fed or have rest, and will anticipate those times well. A routined baby becomes a routined toddler, who becomes a routined child. And routined children are a lot less fussy and a lot more willingly obedient, because they understand that there is a time and a place for everything. "It's not snack time yet," is enough of a reason not to get a biscuit now, and "It's nap time," is enough of a reason to climb onto your bed and fall asleep.

A final word on routines is that, even for babies, a routine that is broken once or twice a week is not a train smash. Babies are given as a blessing to us, not as a ball and chain. There are many things that are more important than your baby's routine, and should be treated as such. If this is your first baby, you might not think so, but one day it will be more important to watch your firstborn's first swimming gala than to be home for your third baby's naptime. It is more important to enjoy special family gatherings, and to be present at certain friends' birthday parties.

> If ever you needed to be part of something bigger than your own life, it is now.

And imperatively, if you are a Christian, it is more important to remain a part of Christian gatherings during this time. If ever you needed to be part of something bigger than your own life, it is now. You are likely to be reading the bible and praying on your own far less than you used to, and it is essential to receive the encouragement and 'watering' that comes from fellowship with other Christians. You'll need two things at least – a time of being taught and hearing God's word, and a time of fellowship.

So make your way to the mother's room or cry room if your church has one, and DON'T sit and chat to the other moms – this is teaching time, not fellowship time – turn up the volume and tune in as far as it is in your power. If your church has no facility, or it is just not conducive to listening, despite your best efforts, then work your baby's routine on that day so that he is sleeping during the preaching time, and sit at the back with him, where you can slip out if he wakes up and becomes a disturbance. As your baby gets older, there are many quiet toys and snacks that might hold his attention during this time: a cardboard book, a soft ball that doesn't roll too well, foam bath animals, raisins, cereals like Oatees or Cornflakes, and a bottle of water. These things are also non-messy if they get spilled.

And then make a plan to be part of a smaller group, preferably with your husband so that your friendships draw you together, and enjoy being a grownup once a week. Let your group encourage you, feel like a contributing member of society by being there for your friends, too, and even let your husband (and yourself) see that you do still remember how to get dressed out of your pyjamas and do your make-up, even if it is just one evening a week! It is great for your baby to learn that his camp-cot or pram is also a 'sleep place' and going to someone else's home on a weekly basis could actually benefit your baby's sleep training, allowing you to be a lot more flexible with taking him out at night to other events. Alternatively, you could always try hosting your group at your house, even if you are not leading it. That way, you can put your baby to sleep in his normal routine, and it has the added benefit that you will be motivated to get your home presentable once a week.

Napping

When you enter into this season of being a mom, you need to come to terms with the fact that your life is no longer on a seven-day cycle, or even a 24-hour cycle, like other working adults. You do not get a day off a week, you do not get annual leave, you do not even get to work just a 15-hour day and then skip the night-shift. However, before you start to feel too sorry for yourself, you do get many opportunities in the day when your baby is sleeping, and if you're wise you will capitalise on those opportunities. If you're very wise, you will be able to make sure that this continues for years.

Newborn babies are on a two-and-a-half to three-hour cycle, and now, so are you. Figure out how many hours of sleep you need in twenty-four (they say five hours MINIMUM), and work out what other activities and tasks you'd like to get done, and then fit them into the three-hour cycles throughout the day and week. Things might shift a little. You might fit in a shower once every eighteen hours instead of twice a day, or you might check your emails once in seven days rather than seven times in one day. You will definitely not get in eight hours of sleep in the night, so work out what are good nap times during the day and it is very possible that you might still get eight hours in twenty-four.

The most important point I want to emphasise is that a change in your sleep schedule to include day-naps, is not just possible, but preferable. If you are going to try and get by without it, then you are making life unnecessarily difficult for yourself, and consequently for your husband and your family. A tired, crabby woman in the house is not helpful to the already more pressurised environment. By napping, you are not shirking your responsibilities, but being wise with managing your responsibilities. Remember, motherhood is not a sprint, it is a very long marathon. Show your man that you have the foresight to think long-term and to pace yourself. And remember, husbands, a woman who gets enough rest is not only happy, she also has energy, and even a bit of libido!

> Give your family the gift of a happy and healthy YOU!

Between twelve and eighteen months a baby will move from two naps a day, to one nap a day. During this time, it is ideal to try and synchronise your baby's naps with your toddler's/children's naps. When he is still on two naps a day, let his morning nap be as early as possible, at his very first indication of tiredness. Very often after having breakfast and maybe having a fun bath and getting dressed, an older baby will be quite happy to give in to his morning sleepiness. I know even for me, that early morning nap can be the best sleep time. Then after lunch you can get the baby down for an afternoon nap together with the rest of the family.

Toddlers and young children should not be allowed to drop their afternoon nap too quickly. My five year old children still nap every afternoon, and once they're at school, my children still nap on any afternoon that they don't have extra-murals. In prep school (senior primary) the homework schedule is a bit heavy... but on weekends they will nap both days if we're home. If it's holiday-time and every afternoon is free, I will allow my school-aged children to nap every second day. But whether they're sleeping or not, after lunch is a time when the house is quiet and everyone is in their rooms, either reading or playing quietly, or resting. I see no reason why this needs to change as the kids get older. Naps are good for all of us.

Like many of the good disciplines in our life, this is not a punishment for the children, but a routine that is good and helpful. I have found my children of all ages infinitely more pleasant and obedient and happy when they are having regular rests.

Particularly when they are in primary school, their lives are very busy and stimulating and demanding. Giving them downtime to think and process their days enables them to cope a lot better with the demands on them. It allows them to consolidate the things they have learnt at school. It gives them time to process the emotional highs and lows of immature friendships and relationships with a huge range of people, from teachers, peers, seniors, juniors, siblings, and parents. Their exposure to diverse people and situations can only be beneficial if they have enough time to think and formulate questions and opinions. If our children keep going, going, going, and even their recreation time is filled with stimulation of TV's, games, and people, they will be bundled along with popular opinions, forced to tumble along with the flow and unable to stand up for what they believe. They will have had no time to assess their tastes, opinions, and beliefs. Rest-time is essential both for sleep and for time alone, and the brain will make the most of whichever of these is necessary if we provide the opportunity. Help your older children to see the benefits of a daytime rest and prompt them in the various ways they might make the most of it, whether it is sleeping, or reading the bible, or thinking, or imagining and inventing.

And once you have managed to get the whole household settled and quiet, accept that you are doing your best for the family by having a rest. It will up your productivity, your mood, your energy, your patience, and your enjoyment of this beautiful season of life.

Fussy Eating

For maximum enjoyment of our children and to avoid bringing up spoiled kids that no one can please, we need to get certain things right from the start. Having good habits and disciplines with our babies is helpful both for ensuring that they are easy and a pleasure now, and that long term it is not a bane to have them in our families.

Some of these good habits are around eating and table manners. From your baby's first spoon-fed meal, he should be taught not to be fussy and spoiled, and that you are in charge, not him. If you are panicking that he is not eating enough, and rushing around trying to please him, you are allowing him to rule the roost.

Offer your baby one choice per meal. When you allow him as much 'mains' as he wants and then follow it with a yoghurt or pureed fruit for dessert, you are walking on dangerous ground. If he knows there is always something sweeter after this meal, why not skip straight to it? Rather let him be sitting either for a savoury meal, or for a snack of fruit/yoghurt. That way, when he fusses that he's finished with this taste, then he's finished with this meal, and can be excused from the table.

It is not your responsibility to ensure that the quantity your baby eats is sufficient. You are in charge of the nutritional value of the food, and he is in charge of the amounts. He knows how much he needs and he would never starve himself. Learning not to take your child's responsibilities onto yourself will go a LONG way to keeping you sane for your entire parenting season.

Good eating habits have got to take location into account. I can assure you, your friends and family, and even the adoring grannies, do NOT want your children walking around their houses with sticky, dirty hands and melting chocolate biscuits, spilling crumbs and tipping juice bottles upside down.

With sleep training, we give our babies safe places that they know they're allowed to sleep in, and when they're in those places they are allowed to have their dummies and blankies and doodoo-cloths. They associate their cots, and prams, and camp-cots and car seats with sleep.

Similarly, we show them which places are eating places – their high chairs, the kiddies' table, a particular mat/towel that can be taken along with you to church or granny's house, the lawn outside, etc. We sit them down for their food, and when they are insisting that they want to crawl off the mat, or climb out the highchair, then their meal is over. If they cry for their food then they are put back into their chair to eat again.

Once they are out of their chair for a minute or two, then the food should be cleared away. This will prevent grazers that want to snack all day, and help our children to understand the routine of daily meals. From a few-months-old to when your kids are all grown, three main meals a day, with a mid-morning and mid-afternoon snack, and a milk breastfeed or bottle for the babies at bed-time, is sufficient and healthy. Anything more will result in unhealthy snacking and will make it difficult for your child to form healthy eating habits as an adult. Once Mom is no longer peeling and slicing fruit and offering an endless supply of Provita's and raisins, they will be forced to resort to fast snacks like chocolate bars and chips.

Finally, in terms of healthy eating habits, for as long as it is possible and reasonable try to delay introducing your child to juice. A little bit of fruit juice is not unhealthy, but it makes getting them to drink water very difficult. Babies and young children drink a lot throughout the day, and you really want them to enjoy water. It is far healthier for their bodies and for their teeth, and is much less of a stress if they're spilling down their shirts and on the floor, which is helpful for being a welcome guest without that juice-bottle-tipping issue!

Time with Your Baby

In order to have this incredible understanding of your baby, and to truly know him, it is necessary to spend as much time with him as possible. I am so desperately aware of the sensitive issues surrounding being a stay-at-home mom versus going back to work, and far be it from me to pass judgment on your unique situation, but it would be amiss of me if I didn't explain the benefits I have had with the incredible privilege of staying at home. To give you a recommendation from my heart, I can only advise you in the way I would advise my little sister, whom I love more than life. Do WHATEVER it takes to secure time at home with your baby. Sell your car, sell your house, change your food, change your lifestyle, but most importantly, change your mind.

We have been brought up to measure our value by our paycheck, and our usefulness by our job title. Just give God a chance, for both you and your spouse, to help you understand how you can best achieve your purpose in this life. Ask him to show you how the two of you are one, and how together, with different roles, you can achieve so much more.

I have to admit that when I was pregnant with my first child, I did not have an overwhelming conviction that I should consider mothering a full-time job. I had heard that it was best, but it was more God's timing and my husband's wisdom that caused me to find myself resigning as an electronic engineer after a recent promotion, and breastfeeding 24-7.

I have never been more grateful, for with each passing year, I look back and wonder how I could possibly have lived with missing all the things I got to witness and enjoy because I was home. I just loved hearing my baby making noises in the next room, and being able to picture her facial expressions exactly because I had spent so much time staring at her.

When I was loaned a breast pump and taught how to prepare a 'freedom bottle' so that I could have a morning or an afternoon to myself without my baby, I just couldn't bring myself to use it. I figured if God thought that the baby and me needed time apart then he wouldn't have created her so completely dependent on me. Breastfeeding is a perfectly designed transition from being permanently attached by an umbilical cord, to being able to release the apron strings altogether. Truth be told, I breastfed for a year just so I could have a good excuse to keep my baby to myself.

I remember a friend telling me how she had gone to her toddler's crèche with the exciting news that he had taken his first steps that weekend. The lady at the crèche looked at her in confusion and said her boy had been walking for weeks. She called him over and he came walking along, but when he saw his mother he dropped and crawled the rest of the way! He was just being a typical manipulative little toddler, getting lots of up-time from his mommy, but it broke my heart that she could have missed his milestone so completely.

I know it's a big decision and I know it's not easy, and I assure you I understand that there are many implications to a mom staying at home. I place high value on a mom being satisfied and happy and I know that, for many people, they feel they can only get that by doing certain jobs that stimulate and excite them, and give them a sense of self-worth and fulfillment. But I also know that hindsight has 20-20 vision, and I have never met a mom who regretted her decision to stay at home with her children, or to look at earning possibilities that allowed her to be home.

Back Yourself

Have you, like me, found it intimidating to hear about all the fine motor skills and gross motor skills and communication skills and whatever else it is that children should be learning at all the appropriate moments? I know when I looked into finding a preschool for my first child it was because I knew that I needed to leave bringing up children to the professionals! There were so many important milestones and I was bound to miss them and damage my precious child for life. So I thought.

And then for some reason, God challenged me about my responsibility to bring up my own children, not that I should exclusively be teaching them necessarily, but that it was my job to monitor milestones and use the aid of teachers where I deemed appropriate.

So I took a shaky stand against the pressure of the 'expected', that told me that I was unable to teach my children to swim, when I am perfectly capable of swimming and have access to a swimming pool, or to 'play ball' when I at least know more than my four-year-old about ball skills, or to dance, or to play piano, or to develop the appropriate gross and fine motor skills, and so on, and so on.

I searched on google for 'preschool milestones' and made sure my kids were doing ok. There is a great website called http://www.shirleys-preschool-activities.com which sent me a weekly e-mail with some activities I could do with my children. And as I watched my kids play, I realised that 'they' made up those milestone lists by watching kids, not by teaching them! Kids' play naturally progresses as they grow! You can't stop a kid from crawling under the dining-room table and over the couch, so why do you have to send them to someone else to build them an obstacle course? They beg to watch you cook, and to help you stir - it doesn't have to be a preschool activity to learn to bake. They practice their fine motor skills eating raisins at snack time!

My kids love making bubblegum out of their marshmallows - you keep breaking and playing with and stretching your marshmallow until it is gooey and stretchy like gum - a trick I taught them that I used to play as a girl. That should develop some serious finger muscles (and it's very easy to wash off hands).

You need to choose which jobs in your home you want to hire out, and which you will keep as your privilege. Will you hire out playing with your children, teaching them to swim, teaching them to catch, teaching them to draw and cut along a line, or will you do those jobs yourself, which might leave you with some extra money to pay someone to cook dinner while you play cricket, or to have your shopping delivered to your doorstep, while you are teaching your kids to draw with chalk on the driveway?

The trick to keeping up with the milestones is to try and say 'Yes' to as many of the activities your children ask to do as possible. Don't stop them climbing on the furniture (when you have given them permission), playing in the mud, sorting their toys into groups that you might think are messy but they think make sense. Let them cut, let them help you cook, let them choose what goes into the trolley, and talk, talk, talk to them all the time, explaining to them everything you do and why, so that they can start to think and reason like an adult.

And while you're teaching them those lesser skills, you will be instilling in them a sense of security and love that you can't pay anyone else to do!

The important thing when taking the risk of parenting into your own hands is to back yourself. God has entrusted you with this job, so you need to trust yourself. Remember, He has equipped you with everything you need, if not within yourself, then within the community He has placed you. James 1:5 "If any of you of you lacks wisdom, he should ask God, who gives generously to all without finding fault, and it will be given to him."

Enjoy it!

When spending time with your baby, don't neglect to smile. From when they are born, until when they are adults, let their picture of you be one with a smile on your face. Whenever your baby catches your eye, whenever you look up from what you are doing because your toddler has called your name, whenever your child spots you waiting in the school car park, whenever your teen walks through the door, SMILE. Let your children feel that you always have time for them, that you delight in them, that you enjoy their company. I have a gorgeous friend called Nix, and the most common memory I have of her with her boys is her laugh. She laughs with them and at them, and at herself, and at life, and her boys are happy children with wonderful senses of humour, that know they are deeply loved and cherished. How wonderful to know that your parents like you and enjoy being with you.

When I had my first baby I received a piece of advice from an older mommy friend of mine. It is really important when you are entering a new season, and in fact in all of life, to have friends that are ahead of you that are open to sharing their successes and failures with you. This friend of mine, Wendy, had two beautiful girls at the time, and they were already growing up so fast. Wendy said to me, "If there's one thing I could pass on, it would be 'hold them while you can'!" Babies and children grow up so fast, and soon your arms will be empty. Whenever it catches your fancy, laugh off all the rules and wisdom of not spoiling your kids and gather them into your arms for as long as they will stay there.

> Keep friends that are slightly ahead of you in their parenting season that you can learn from.

11 BRINGING UP WARRIORS

I was pushing Superman around in a trolley the other day at the supermarket, and when I added Oros to my other groceries he told me I was a good boy... Oh, the joy of being mom to a two-year-old! His Superman suit has built-in padded muscles, but they only work to carry a box of cornflakes in from the car - anything else is too heavy.

It amazes me how a little boy is so keen to be a strong protector. When I told my three year old boy to come and sit on the couch with me because I was going to read to him about how to build roads, he said, "I can build roads, Mom. I can build roads for you!"

If he sees me carrying a bag he asks if he can carry it, because "It's too heavy for you, Mom." If he forgets his little bicycle outside after tidy-up time, he insists on coming with me in the dark to bring it in, so he "can look after me". He is now four, and he's teaching his two year old brother to open the car doors for their older sisters. Amazing, how manners can be taught so young and how receptive and eager to please our little men are!

When it comes to bringing up boys it is important, particularly for moms (and female teachers), to keep the desired outcome in mind. These boys need to become men who know they've got what it takes, who back themselves in a game, or in war, who are wild enough to be effective, and wise enough to be gentle. They need to know how to wield a weapon, be it a gun, or a cricket bat, or their tongue, or their wallet, and yet they need to be respectful enough of life to wield their weapons only as a last resort. They must love to shoot, but hate to kill, love to compete and to win, but love more to play the game.

I remember the awe I felt when my first son was born. I didn't know how to mother him because I felt like I was nursing someone who was bigger than me. It actually took me a while to bond with my baby - it was like I was nurturing a cub that would turn into a lion! After a week or two, though, he started to coo, and I realised he was just a cute little baby!

Still, when a woman is mothering a boy, she needs to keep in mind that she is bringing up a warrior that is different from her in function, and she needs to smother him with kisses, and then let go and let him run, all in the same day.

Desired Outcome

Who is it that God is wanting your son to become? What will some of the roles and functions be that he will need to fulfil?

He will need to be a provider. He needs to know his responsibilities and be diligent and hard-working. Our little boys should not sit around reading comic books when their dads are washing the car outside or their moms are carrying in the groceries. We need to instill in them the privilege that it is to be strong and capable and teach them to apply their strength.

They need to understand the responsibility they have to study and learn, with the spelt out purpose of being able to buy their children food, and bicycles, and to be able to care for poor people who didn't have the privilege of going to school.

He will need to be a protector. Help him to be brave and to back himself in a fight. DO NOT give him your fears of spiders, or dirt, or heights, or baddies. He needs to understand dangers, of course, but because he is wise not because he is weak. A man should not seek out danger, but neither should he fear it.

He will need to be a warrior. Don't shush him all the time! Boys are loud, and wild, and fast! That's the way we want them. The boundaries we give them MUST be big enough to allow them to grow bigger than a Bonsai!

But of course, he should be taught to be respectful and considerate, to be gentle with the young and the weak, and considerate to the old and the fussy. We must teach our boys that their strength and energy is a gift that comes with responsibilities and needs to be managed.

He will need to be a husband, lover and father. While it is important to allow boys to be boys, we don't need to panic when they are wanting to play with baby dolls, or to be lovey-dovey and affectionate. Again, when we think of our 'end product', we definitely want men who see value in being nurturing and loving and romantic and don't see it as beneath them or beyond them.

I do, however, aim to put my boys off dressing up with make-up and nail polish. When they see their big sisters or Mommy doing these things and they feel left out, I remind them of the fun things only boys get to do - like walk around without a shirt on and shave your face and wee in the garden. Life's not fair, but we need to make the most of who we are and what we have.

Daddy the Hero

Well done, Daddy,
Well done, Daddy,
Well done, Daddy,
You got us home again!

You're our hero!
You're the best,
You're Super-Dad,
Super-super Dad!

We're just turning into our driveway after another long car trip, and we're celebrating how Daddy has done it again. Our boys need role models, and who better than their Dads?

Our boys 'rate' themselves as being the strongest, bravest, and fastest in the world. I have been told by them that they're "faster than wildebeests", "stronger than lions", and "braver than monkeys". (Don't ask me – I'm just quoting their words!) I have even been told that they're "not scared of swimming with crocodiles... but only small ones... and only when they're dead!"

But if there's one thing they'll concede it's that Dad is stronger than them, and Jesus is stronger than Dad!

We need to be constantly celebrating Daddy's noble, manly deeds (and of course Mommy's, for girls). Point out to your sons and your daughters how Daddy works hard to provide, how good he is at catching a ball, how big his muscles are, how kind he is to Mommy, what a good Daddy he is to the baby, how he protects us by locking the house, how he drives the family well and carefully, how he carries heavy things. The Daddy in our family is not perfect, and neither is the Mommy. But we need to highlight the many, many things that we want our children to imitate one day, and to look for in choosing a spouse.

Boys and Blood

I just adore the way boys were born to be wild. When my boy was three, I was pregnant, so was not very good at helping him learn to ride his bicycle. It's difficult enough to run after them, bent in half holding the bike, when you're not pregnant! So, my darling son was being 'marginalised', and spent many hours a day on the driveway, riding with his ferry wheels on... so I thought. I went to sit outside and watch him one day, and there he was, riding down the driveway, on his own, without his training wheels.

"Oh my word, my boy! When did you learn to ride? Who took your side wheels off?"

"I did. Watch me, Mom!"

I ran inside to get the video camera and came out to film the monumental occasion, which had obviously happened a few days earlier without being recorded!

The best part was when I watched how he stopped - by crashing into a concrete pillar that is lying horizontal on the grass, waiting to be erected. On closer inspection of the pillar, I found it to be covered in dried blood, from the last few weeks of teaching himself to ride (though clearly, he had not yet mastered braking, so at least I had something left to teach him!)

How do you help your boys not to be crybabies when it comes to hurting themselves, while at the same time not being insensitive, and reverting back to the faulty old way of 'big boys don't cry'?

I think firstly, that tears have a place when you are experiencing something (sadness, pain) that is difficult to put into words. So a baby can cry when he's hungry, but a toddler should say, "Ta num num" if he is able to. Similarly a young child may cry when he's hurt himself, but he should be learning that the correct response is, "Ow! That was sore." When my children come crying to me with a minor injury, I give them a hug, but I also remind them to 'use their words' to tell me what's wrong.

Of course it's easier to teach them when they're not crying, so when they're heading out the door to play, remind them, "Remember, big boy, when you hurt yourself, you don't need to run and tell me. Just say 'Ow! That was sore!', and carry on playing. Later, when you are finished playing, you can come and tell me what happened and show me your new sores, ok?"

When they do come and show me, blood is celebrated. "Well done, my boy! You've got blood! You're such a strong, brave boy! You can show Daddy when he gets home!"

In the same way, we show off our own little bumps and bruises, especially if Daddy gets hurt doing something manly, like woodwork, or indoor cricket. "Wow, Daddy also has blood! Well done, brave Daddy! Did you cry?"

"No, I just said 'Ow!' and kept on playing cricket, boy. But it was really, really sore, so inside, I was going, 'Ow, ow, ow, ow!' And jumping up and down like this!" (Come on, demonstrate. Show your kids you're also just a little boy on the inside!)

You need to get your older kids, caregivers etc on board with this for it to work. There's no use if the overly maternal big sister picks up the crying toddler, and loves all over him while cooing that she will carry him to Mommy. That type of smothering attention only reinforces your toddler behaving like a baby.

I know how much a mommy adores her little babies, and how we wish to keep them from any pain, but may I please suggest that it is unwise to offer Panado for a scraped knee? The everyday pain that life brings us can be coped with in many better ways before medicine is a necessary alternative.

Must Boys Fight?

I have been asked about boys and fighting - where do you draw the line? Are they allowed to defend themselves?

Boys will be boys, right? ...Right... but they need not be bullies or brats. Boys love to wrestle. In fact, ironically, as I started writing this section, I was interrupted for an on-the-kitchen-floor-wrestle and pile-on by my two year old and four year old boys. (I was at the bottom for most of it. They have an unfair advantage when they attack in two's.)

So first off, I think we all seem to agree these days that boys need to be allowed to be physical and play rough games. Our wrestling does sometimes include kisses and cuddles in between the overthrowing and pinning down... I know, I know, it's not very 'manly' but I'm the mom, not the dad, so I'm allowed.

My boys' fighting is governed by certain rules - first, in accordance with the family rule that we must always respect one another, (and each other's bodies), you must first ask before wrestling with someone. "Can I wrestle you?" or "Can we play 'fighting'?"

Secondly, a call for "Mercy" must always be honoured. If at any moment someone taps out, or cries, "Mercy", or says they've had enough, the wrestle needs to be immediately ended.
This applies to grownups, too! Daddies, and uncles and grampa's are notorious for their tickling and teasing and throwing into the pool. This plays a wonderful role in toughening up your children, teaching them to fend for themselves and to understand relationships that are different to the nurturing that they are used to, and shouldn't be stopped too early. However, when a child calls for mercy, we need to make sure they get it. When you know your child is being serious, and an adult thinks that to carry on would be fun, it is reasonable and kind for you to defend your child in a courteous way.

Thirdly, you are never allowed to wrestle or fight when you're angry. Which brings us to the question: "In a fight, where do you draw the line? Are they allowed to defend themselves?"
I draw the line right at the beginning. I find for little people, who are still in training, that's the best place to draw it. In other words, it is never ok to use violence to settle an argument, even if it is in retaliation. Ask yourself, "How do I want my boys to respond when they are young men? What am I training them for?" I can assure you, I would be horrified if my husband threw a punch in anger, no matter how much 'the other guy' deserved it.
What would I expect of a Godly man who has been hurt or mistreated? I would expect him to follow the biblical way set out for adults when they disagree - that is, speak to the person who has wronged you, and if you are unable to come to an agreement, then go together to a higher authority - in this case, your mom.
So, the training goes:

Rourke (2yrs): "That my wheelbarrow!"
Jed (4yrs): Ignores him.
Rourke: Screams or (occasionally) hits Jed
Jed: "Mom! Rourke hit me!!"

Me: "I'm sorry Rourke hit you. But my Jed, you were ignoring Rourke. That is rude manners to ignore someone. Remember, we get smacks for disrespecting people in this family. And Rourke, you must just ask nicely if you want your wheelbarrow, see? We always talk nicely to each other. You are going to get a smack, Rourkie, 'cos you screamed and hit Jed. We don't hit people."

I apply my Three D's to this situation, that is 1. Disobedience, 2. Disrespecting people, 3. Disrespecting property, to establish which offenses are smack-worthy.

So in this scenario, my principles for discipline would be: shouting or speaking rudely to someone is disrespectful, so that would get a smack. That may be harsh to some, but it results in children who very seldom fight, and most often speak respectfully to each other, even if they are arguing over something - to me, that's worth it; ignoring someone intentionally is disrespectful, also a smack; snatching is disrespectful, smack; hitting someone in anger is definitely disrespectful, smack; telling on is not allowed, but it was neither done in disrespect or in disobedience, so it doesn't get a smack, it gets a reminder, "My boy, you can't come and tell me what happened when you haven't spoken to Rourke yet. You must say to Rourke, 'Rourkie boy, don't smack me please. That is sore and I don't like it.' If Rourke won't listen to you then you can bring him to me."

So, do my children fight? Yes, sure they do. I expect them to. They're still in training, remember? But what I expect, and what I ask for, are two different things. So without being surprised, or shocked, or disappointed, I am constantly reminding them to talk respectfully to one another, to ask nicely, to treat each other with respect... And I am pleased to encourage you with this - they can actually do it most of the time! Training works!

There are two helpful keys to the success of this training. Firstly, the rules must be constantly upheld. The children must know that you have eyes and ears everywhere, and that you always expect the same respectful behaviour towards each other. And secondly, you need to be around to do the training. Between, say, eighteen months and around four or five years old, a child needs to be trained. Trained does not mean smacked, it means taught, reminded, constantly. I am with my children most of the day, every day. I am constantly reminding them, "Careful, my boy, how do we ask?", "Your brother is talking to you, my boy, don't ignore him.", "When you want something, you must ask and put out your hand flat like this. Don't snatch. Wait for them to give it to you."

Isn't it incredible that it is within our power as parents to determine whether or not our children will enjoy each other's company? All I can say is, give your children the gift of friendship. Teach them how to respect and honour one another, and it will go well in your home!

12 WHAT A GIRL NEEDS

Ah, girls! The beauty and the mystery! Not even being one will guarantee that you understand them. Like a flower, they can withstand a thunderstorm and an earthquake, and yet be destroyed by a breeze.

If there is one thing to bringing up girls, it is the essential importance of 'observant and intentional parenting'. It tests our 'whale watching' skills to the max. While a little boy wants to know if he's got what it takes to be a man, a little girl wants to know that she is seen, and she is found beautiful.

If you could take the word 'cherish' and put it into action, you would have what every girl needs. To 'cherish' is to have time for, to hold delicately, and to think highly of. To cherish someone is to feel honoured to have the privilege of loving them and the joy of knowing them.

A little girl needs to know that her mom is not in competition with her, but is one of her fans. She needs to know that her mom values their relationship and loves to spend time with her.

My daughter once spoke to me with an attitude that was disrespectful and unbecoming of a lady. I was in two minds about how to discipline her, because she is starting to grow up and I think there comes an age where spankings are inappropriate and less effective. However, for her, they were still the discipline tool that resulted in the most change, and I really wanted to nip this attitude in the bud.

A little while later we had a chance to chat. I explained to her how much I valued our relationship and how precious she was to me. I told her of how I longed for years of being friends with her, and for that reason, even though I hated smacking her, I was willing to do it if that's what it took to make sure that things like disrespect, or lying, ever threatened to come between us. By the end of our chat she was beaming with pride, and I heard her boasting to her sister in the next room that mom wanted to be best friends with her!

A little girl's relationship with her dad is very important and incredibly consequential. Apparently, healthy physical contact with her dad, like wrestling, or piggybacks, or sitting on his lap, can actually delay the onset of puberty! A little girl's body will be aware that she is already in a relationship with a man who can protect her, and provide for her, and love her, and so find it unnecessary to rush into developing sexually in order to get those needs fulfilled.

Senseless Sensitivities

Little girls are incredibly sensitive. From my experience, they want to please you perfectly, all the time, and it is heartbreaking for them when they feel they have failed or don't measure up. They are not reasonable in their ability to see that it might be outside circumstances that are causing your impatience, or that you might still love them, even when you are expressing disappointment in them.

I still remember so clearly when I was trying to climb on to my dad's lap, and he was trying to unwind and watch the news after a hard days work. He brushed me off, saying "Not now," while looking over my head at the TV. Looking back I can totally understand that I was interrupting, and can see how he always gave me hours and hours of attention, but at the time I felt rejected.

I remember the time my mom was not in the mood to have to kiss a plastic doll goodnight and I was so upset I refused to let her kiss me goodnight either. She came to me afterwards and begged for another chance to kiss both the doll and me.

Looking back at both of these scenarios I can see that I was being unreasonably sensitive and yet it strikes me that I remember them because they were important to me at the time. Golly, girls are sensitive, and as parents we're bound to get things wrong with them some times. We need to be aware of their sensitivities, but also, and VERY importantly, we need to make sure that we don't always indulge them and bring up spoiled princesses that are painfully high maintenance for their husbands!

Most of the time it is enough for them just to have their feelings acknowledged, as I remember both my parents thoughtfully did for me. That doesn't mean letting the brat behaviour go unpunished. Our girls must learn that it is their responsibility to communicate reasonably when they have been hurt, and to understand that they are not always the centre and reason for everybody else's behaviour. Sometimes people are just tired and need a break.

We need to teach them not to take themselves so seriously and to laugh at themselves. Share with them when you mess up and help them to see how you work through the emotions of deciding whether to be embarrassed and humiliated or whether to laugh at yourself. Yip, bringing up kids means doing a lot of work on ourselves because they're probably going to learn only the lessons that you have already mastered! We need to grow up if we want to bring up kids!

I guess I just gave my little girl a sad story to remember about me - she was doing her first project for school and had innovatively decided to add in a map of South Africa. Apparently it was not the right thing for me to ask her why she had drawn a butternut in her project about sugar cane. The butternut was supposed to be South Africa, and it was orange because she had found an outdated map that read "Orange Free State". I didn't make it better when that made me laugh!

But laughing at ourselves and at each other is not always malicious. In fact, among family and friends, it is usually because they love us that they laugh. We just need to learn to join in! Point out how we laugh when the baby is trying to walk or the toddler makes a cute error in his speech. We are all still learning things, and if we feel like a failure when we don't get it right, we may as well not bother to come out our rooms. Reassure your children that you love them completely even though they're not perfect. Teach them to see the funny side of tripping on stage at speech day, and remember, they're watching you to determine what emotions are appropriate.

Intimacy

A mommy friend of mine, Wendy, told me of a special place in her home where she had instituted an immunity zone. She had a special window seat in her main bedroom, and if the children wanted to talk to her about something private, or to tell her something without getting into trouble, they could request a visit on this 'honesty bench'.

It is important for our children, and particularly our girls, to feel that they are safe to talk to us about anything. We like to take our girls on 'chat dates', which is when one of us will take one of our daughters on a special outing, and talk about anything and everything. We have been to restaurants, and coffee shops, to a small local airport to watch the planes taking off, and for walks along the beach. We chat openly and honestly, and have been asked the most delightful questions.

If you want to have an open relationship with your teenager, where they feel comfortable to talk to you about anything, you need to start young. Their conversation might seem irrelevant and even annoying to you, but it means everything to them. When they are complaining about the same friend or the same problem at school for the hundredth time, and it all seems so obvious and ridiculous to you, you better know it is life and death to them.

Developing trust takes time, and patience, and it takes getting onto their level. Very often it takes seeking God for an answer to their questions, and how lovely if you can do that together with your daughter?

When our daughters feel that we are understanding and not condescending, that we value our time with them and take them seriously, they will have no problem to consider us both disciplinarian parent, and trusted friend. The two are not mutually exclusive, as we so often hear. God manages to be both, and He can help us to be both to our children, too.

Be a Model

Mothers need to live out loud in front of their daughters, and be a model to them of a wife, a mother, a friend and a daughter. If you have no time for your own mom or mom-in-law, you can legitimately fear that your daughters might emulate that one-day. Point out the ways in which you respect and honour your parents even into adulthood, and teach them how to phone Granny and Grampa with all their news.

When your daughter asks you why Daddy has not yet done the home maintenance or chores that you asked him to, teach her about how a "nagging wife is like a dripping tap" (Proverbs 19:13) and how it is better to "live on your roof than to share a house with a quarrelsome wife" (Proverbs 21:9). Point out the ways in which you love and serve your husband and teach them that it is a delight.

Explain to them your parenting decisions, and why they're not necessarily parented the same as some other children in their class. Show them the consequences of various parenting styles, and why you are loving them by bringing them up in a certain way.

Fathers are a model to their daughters of what kind of husband they should choose one day. I am often pointing out the incredibly noble qualities in my husband, and suggesting to my daughters that it might be wise if they allow us to help them in finding a husband as good as their dad. I warn them of the power of love, and how we can be blinded by flattery and attention. We make lists of things a man should be in order to be a good choice as a husband and father.

When this is instilled at a young age, it is not forgotten. While our daughters might indulge in a season of wandering and exploring things in their own way, they will know in their hearts that when a big decision needs to be made they should resort to the wisdom that they were taught as children.

Gentle Doesn't Mean Weak

There is nothing more beautiful and captivating and alluring than a woman who understands femininity. A gentle lady-like posture will set your daughter apart. Practice being a lady yourself, and teach her feminine ways. Encourage her in ballet, and gentle speech and girlish charm.

Compliment her when she has put together an outfit that has feminine taste and style. Of course it won't be perfect, but pick out the things that you would like to see more of, and you will find that 'what we celebrate, we generate'. Teach her about patterns that clash and colour tones that don't work well together. When she has made a special effort to dress like a lady and to accessorise her outfit, give her a compliment. It will make her day that you noticed and that you had the time to say something kind. Compliments from both Mommy and Daddy are essential, each for their own reasons. Nothing boosts a girl's confidence more than a special compliment from her daddy. He is the man in her life, and considering her unsure journey of discovering herself, a young girl needs even more 'noticing' than the mom/wife.

But don't make the mistake of allowing her to think she is weak. Encourage her that she can ride bikes, and play lawn cricket with the best of them. If it is not her primary talent, encourage her to keep at it anyway, so that she will not be left out of sporty games her whole life. Help her to understand that she is still young and she has years of beach volleyball, and social tennis, and active games ahead of her that she would be devastated to be excluded from for the sake of vanity or laziness.

Your girls should not be excluded from having to carry in bags from the car, and help Daddy in his latest woodwork project, just as your boys should not be excluded from household chores.

Remember that you are raising WOMEN, and wives and mothers, and these jobs are not for sissies! Emotional and physical weakness will get them nowhere in life. Display your inner strength to them, and keep your complaining and grumbling to yourself, and encourage them that though life may be tough sometimes, even at their age, they have strength both within themselves from God, and within God that is available to them.

> We are raising **women**, and wives and mothers. These jobs are not for sissies!

My girls are often heard to say, "This is tough, but I can do it." Phrases like that are taught and modeled and repeated, so that their inner thoughts are guided in helpful ways when they need them.

It is not too much to ask for emotional stability and maturity from them, especially when we are sympathetic to the self-discipline it may require at times. Communicate with your children and help them to process their emotions.

"You feel so frustrated right now, and that's fine. It is even okay to be mad at me sometimes. But you must be respectful even when you are frustrated. You can't just sulk or grump around the house. It is not everybody else's fault that you are mad. Come to me if I upset you and say, 'Mom, you hurt me by saying that. You made me feel stupid/sad/angry.' "

Just as we had to equip our toddlers with the words to ask for water and food and toys, so we have to equip our children and our pre-teens with the words to express their emotions in a mature and honouring way. And of course, we need to hold ourselves to at least the same standard, both with our children, and with our spouses and other relationships!

13 FAMILY PLANNING

Perhaps you want to think twice about taking any family planning leaf out of our book – after all, we are expecting our sixth child! But I assure you that our family has been carefully planned and we are so very satisfied and pleased with our lot.

Richard and I never knew when we were dating or first married that we would have a big family. We didn't have a particular reference for it, and we both came from families of three children. But we knew as we were going that we were not quite done, and now, as we await our fourth little boy's birth, we just know that we have all our 'chickens' in the 'nest'.

Courage to Keep Going

After our first baby girl, we had the sad experience of losing our second baby during pregnancy at the end of her first trimester. Our third pregnancy with our baby boy nearly ended in tragedy as well.

To tell you the story, I am going to use an excerpt from a journal I have kept for him. A friend of mine, Megan, was presented with twenty-one letters from her mother on her twenty-first birthday.

Her mom had written her a letter each year without her knowing, and it was so precious to Meg to see how her mother had felt about her and loved her throughout the years. I thought that was a wonderful idea, so I started a journal for each child, and whenever I have time or something precious to record, I write them a letter in their journal. Please don't tell my children about these journals as I am hoping to present them on their twenty-first birthdays as a surprise. (Although they have been so sweet and interested in my writing, I am counting on them not reading this parenting book until they're much older!)

6 March 2007 (1 day old)

Jed Daniel

My darling boy! Welcome to the world. What a time we have had with you since yesterday morning. We are so grateful to God for sustaining your little life. How frightening it has been. You are currently receiving a blood transfusion... but let me start at the beginning.

I had had mild contractions all weekend and at about 2am on Monday morning they were getting rather sore. At 4am I prayed that my waters would break so that I could know that this was the real thing, and shortly after, they started to trickle out. I was in the bathroom so I tried to call out in a loud whisper to Daddy so as not to wake Jada and Kiara. When he finally heard me he came stumbling to the bathroom in a panic — and then lost the sense of urgency as he kept blinking and took a while to focus his eyes and wake up properly.

We excitedly did last minute preparations to leave the girls at home and gather our things. Daddy phoned your grampa and granny, Papa and GJ to come and look after the girls. By now I was in a lot of pain and struggled to walk to the car and climb in. We finally had to leave before Papa and GJ managed to get there, and just leave the keys in the post box.

Luckily the hospital is only two minutes away. Going over the bumps in the parking lot was so sore! Daddy wheeled me in a wheel chair up to the maternity ward, and the midwife hurried to phone the doctor. We heard her whispering on the phone, "Now... no, no, right now!"

She had me lie on my side to keep you from coming out before the doctor came, and she held my knees closed with one hand and your head in with the other hand. The doctor arrived shortly afterwards and greeted us with a smile, and then hurried to put his gloves on when he saw your head was coming out.

Once I was helped back onto my back, the birthing contractions had become so intense that I couldn't hold you in anymore. The doctor and midwife kept telling me to stop pushing, but I wasn't.

Doctor: "Push... okay, stop! STOP!

Daddy whispered, "His head's out!"
Doctor: "Okay, slowly now. Push. Okay, stop!
Daddy: "He's out!"

The nurse and doctor looked very serious and worried through out, and when they placed you on my chest, we realized something was wrong. You were as white as wax, and limp and silent. The doctor asked if he could take you, and they tried to get you breathing. The doctor and nurse were working on you on a little baby station in the delivery room, and daddy and I were praying and begging you to breathe and cry. After an agonising few minutes you made a quiet little moan, and we thanked God!

The gynae and midwife phoned the paediatrician and rushed you off to ICU High Care, with Daddy following. I was left alone in the delivery room, lying in a pool of fluid, your placenta still undelivered. I was alone for about fifteen minutes, just praying for you to live, and wondering how I would cope if you didn't.

The doctor came back to deliver my placenta. He was halfway through stitching me back up where he had had to cut because you were such a big baby (4kg!), when Daddy came back in tears to say the nurses couldn't get the incubator to work. The doctor rushed to help, then came back to finish stitching me, and then left to check on you again.

By now I was freezing and shaking from lying in all that fluid and from the shock. I couldn't keep my knees still while he was stitching me. While lying on my own I started vomiting. When Daddy came back to tell me the paediatrician had arrived (in his sleeping shorts!) he found me in this state and for a while he was worried he might be losing both of us.

He asked me, "You are going to make it, right?"

And I reassured him I would be fine.

The paediatrician explained to us that you had lost nearly sixty percent of your blood during birth, presumably through a tear in your placenta, and that your remaining blood had turned acidic from the shock. He couldn't guarantee that you would survive, but he warned us that at best you would be in ICU for four to six weeks.

Grampa and our pastor, Peet had arrived and we all went through to High Care to pray for you. You were as pale as anything, and were hooked up to every conceivable tube and monitor. But still, you looked just like your dad! You looked like a rugby player with the little white plaster over the bridge of your nose.

We laid our hands on your still, pale little body and we prayed with all our hearts for your life to be spared and your body to be strengthened.

Right then, as we were praying, your face began to get some pink colour, and it went down your neck and onto your chest. Your grampa was so amazed at this miracle before our eyes.

From then, you just went from strength to strength. The doctors confessed that your first hour of life was completely out of their hands. They didn't know if you would make it. You had so many people praying for your life, and the doctors said that God truly intervened.

My mom (your Doodie) and Uncle Kev arrived and we all sat together in the visitors' lounge because I didn't want to go through to the maternity ward where I would have to be alone. When everyone went home later that day, I tried to sleep, but my arms felt so empty without you. Both the gynae and the paediatrician checked on you all day, and one nurse was allocated just to watch you breathe.

The paediatrician told me to give up hope of feeding you myself because you were too weak and weren't allowed off the machines. However, that very first evening, not twelve hours later, he said I could hold you and try to feed you. I was so excited to hold you for the first time! We tried to feed, and, yet another miracle, you latched on and fed beautifully on both sides – unusual for even a healthy newborn baby! You continued to feed excellently every three *hours through the night, and when the doctor did his morning rounds he was so impressed that he allowed you to be moved to a normal crib – off oxygen and lights and out of High Care.*

...

After every test they could do, they found you in perfect health, and three days after you were born, we were discharged and allowed home!

You are such a special boy and God has given us such a good gift in you. As my friend, Jenni said, what has God in store for you that He had so many people praying for you in your first hours of life?

We love you, boy. Welcome to our family, and welcome home.

So, so, so much love
Your Mummy

While lying in the delivery room on my own, waiting to hear if our little boy was going to live or not, I begged God not to ask me to have any more children if this boy wasn't going to make it. But even as I prayed, I knew that I was not going to let this tragedy rule our lives. God was still good, and His plans were still perfect. I could never turn away from the future he had for us.

Having children takes courage, and for many people, it is surrounded by difficulty and tragedy. When your third IVF fails, or your pregnancy miscarries, when your long awaited baby is stillborn, or you find your precious angel has stopped breathing in his cot, courage may fail you.

But anything so wonderful is worth fighting for, and when you have gotten to the end of your life, you will be grateful for your perseverance. Each child, no matter how prematurely lost, is a gift and a blessing, and your life is the richer for having had them pass through.

What's the Number?

When people visit our home for the first time, or stay for a few days, they often remark how un-chaotic and un-crowded it is. I'm not sure what they expected to find but it's true that our home is full, but not overcrowded.

We have found ourselves wanting to have a big family, and on a practical level, it has been great to feel that our hard work of inputting into our children has a higher productivity rate than if we had fewer of them. Story-time, family outings, educational toys, and everything else, benefits six little future soldiers, not just one or two. It makes decisions like staying at home with them seem more weighty and productive. It feels like good time management of these parenting years, and allows us to shoot more 'arrows' in more directions eventually.

But also, it is just fun to be a part of a big family. Every adult we spoke to that grew up in a bigger family said they loved it. We figured it would be a beneficial thing for our children, and we wanted them to have the same passion and fondness for their family as we witnessed in those we chatted to that had had that privilege. Our decision has been more for their sake, than for realising a particular dream of ours.

I would not have a set number of children to recommend to you, but we do have an opinion on how that number should be established for each family. That is to say that we believe that a couple needs to come to the understanding that children are a blessing, not a burden, and that it is both our privilege, and our responsibility to bring up the next generation.

Psalm 128 (ESV)
Blessed is everyone who fears the Lord, who walks in his ways!
You shall eat the fruit of the labor of your hands;
you shall be blessed, and it shall be well with you.
Your wife will be like a fruitful vine within your house;
your children will be like olive shoots around your table.
Behold, thus shall the man be blessed who fears the Lord.

I think it would be a disaster to look back and have to admit you had one child too many. We have always wanted to maintain a home that is peaceful and ordered, notwithstanding the obvious hard work that comes with raising a young family of any size. It wouldn't do to have a child more than either the father or mother could cope with, understanding of course that our capacity grows with each child, as long as we are growing at a manageable rate! And of course finances need to be considered, with wisdom, but also with creativity and flexibility.

So while we would always recommend carefully thinking about the practicalities of adding a child to your existing family, we also have made each decision with privilege and responsibility foremost in our thinking. Always remember that children are a delight and that we're allowed to have more if we want to! God is a giver of super fantastic gifts and if you and your spouse both want to have more, then go for it. Your friends and your parents, while they might be heavily involved in your children's lives, and therefore be considered in your decision, have had their own chance to plan a family – this is your chance. On the other hand, a gift that you never wanted, like a puppy you can't manage, is a bad gift, and you have no compulsion to have more children if neither of you want to, no matter what the outside pressure.

Also, we need to remember that life is not all about us and our comfort, and if you have not been stirred to have any children, or have been purely selfishly motivated in your family planning, then it might be worth getting before God and asking Him to give you his heart for your family, and sacrificing your comfort and selfishness for His greater purposes. As we have clearly covered, having children is also our responsibility, and perhaps we should be asking God how many we could wisely manage, and then full our capacity with this Godly purpose.

For us, it has been a joy to fill our home, which we feel at the moment we have done, although we are always open to God's surprising promptings. We would advise young families to aim for a full home, bursting with joy and purpose, not to settle for a half-full home, and to be wary of overfilling their home. But what exactly that number is, is dependent on the couple, their personal capacity, and their other responsibilities and pressures, and will be influenced by a number of factors. It is an exciting decision, needing to be carefully weighed up by them and God.

His Ways Are Higher Than Our Ways

When we were expecting our first baby, we had the privilege of visiting a couple whom God had called to plant a church. I remember watching in awe as their two teenage daughters formed such an integral part of what God had called them to, leading worship, gathering teens and families, and just being themselves. It was so very obvious to me that God's calling for them at that particular time was for the whole family, and they could never have fulfilled that purpose as effectively without each member of the family. It struck me how important it was for God to be in charge of your family planning, because he's the only one who knows your family's future. He knows if you will be better with all girls, or all boys, with two, or four, or six, with children made from your ingredients, or with children that are already made and looking for a family.

Let's remember to always be open to God and his prompting, to keep our minds open to adopting and to having a family different from what we imagined. When we are completely submitted to God leading our lives, and willing to be lead anywhere, no matter what others may say, or how unexpected a path we go on, we will succeed in having the perfectly suited children to our family. How exciting to have the one who sees our future able to help us plan!

It goes without saying that where health dictates that we are unable to have children, or to have the family that we had hoped for, we should live in freedom, and without guilt, trusting that His ways are higher than our ways, that His plans for us are good, and that He will work out His specific purpose for our lives.

14 ON A PERSONAL NOTE

I find myself uniquely positioned to be writing a book like this because I'm still having babies, and toddlers, and young children, and I'm still so aware of the demands of this life stage. It hasn't become a rose-tinted memory. And yet I've also got children in Junior and Senior Primary, which has helped me to see how quickly the seasons are passing and how soon our time with our children will be over.

Cherish the Moment

Did it ever occur to you that those grannies are right, and life really is very short? I'm not sure when it happened, but a few years ago it seems like God exploded my mind to allow me to understand a little bit more of eternity and a little bit more of how the decades fly by in this lifetime. Children certainly help us see how quickly time flies. I remember celebrating my first child's first birthday, and saying to my husband, "I can't believe we only get another seventeen of those!"

I feel like I want to hang on to time with both hands to slow it down. Every moment, I'm taking snaps in my mind and hoping I will remember it forever. When my husband gets into bed after I'm asleep, I can't stop myself from reaching out to him, because one day if I don't have him, I will kick myself for the good night kisses I never took when I had the chance. I want to stare at him in the shower, and memorise his body, and cherish the feeling of his arms around me, while I still have them.

I guess this strange way of life was encouraged when an eight-month pregnant friend lost her husband in an instant, and again, when a close friend died of a brain tumour, after being diagnosed just ten days earlier, leaving behind her hubby and a two-year and three-year-old.

Whatever the reason, the result is a huge hard-drive full of photographs, many journals full of cute sayings and memories, and some rather wild decisions to make the most of every moment, so hopefully, even though we only get one short life on Earth, at the end of it I can say that I have 'sucked the marrow out of it', and this strange obsession with the speed of time would have turned out to be a blessing after all!

Hard, hard, hard, hard, hard, hard Work!

We were sitting in a church elders meeting a number of years ago, and it had been a painful season in the church with some of the tragedies and difficulties people had been through. There had also been some tough opposition to some of the work of the church. As we sat in the elders meeting, our leader started off by saying, "Sometimes, ministry is hard, hard, hard, hard..." We started smiling as he continued to list the 'hard's. Each time he was about to finish off his sentence, his mind would recall something else we had dealt with as a team, and he would just shake his head and continue, "...hard, hard, hard, hard, hard, hard work." By the time he was finished, many minutes later, we all had the giggles, although he was being quite serious. Sometimes it's laugh, or cry, right?

It occurs to me that being a grownup is, in itself, pretty hard work. So is being a parent. I just have it on my heart to encourage you not to wish your adulthood away, and particularly, not to wish your children's childhoods away. Changing nappies is tough, but the next season of potty training also has its challenges. Having to get up early to get the baby out the cot in the morning may be annoying, but having the toddler in a bed and able to chose his morning wake-up-time is also difficult. Having young kids with you every second of the day is impossible, but having to do lifts and homework and pay for hockey sticks and rugby boots is equally so.

So rather than wish for the next season, which you might just find has challenges of its own just as difficult as the season you're in, accept the fact that being a grownup is sometimes just hard, hard, hard, hard, hard, hard, hard, hard, hard, hard work. Sometimes it feels like a marathon and you think 'if I can just make it to the finish'... but life is really a journey, not a marathon with an end. Try to focus on the treasures and joys of the season you're in, and remember, it's not what you have, but what you enjoy that counts.

The Secret to Joy

In His last major lesson to His disciples before He dies, Jesus goes on and on about remaining in Him. If we love Him, we must remain in Him. To remain in Him, we must do what He commands. His command is this: love one another. And then He confirms that He is teaching us this so that His joy may be in us and our joy may be complete. When we love one another and lay down our lives for each other, we will find joy (John 15).

It makes more sense to me intellectually that I will be happier buying myself some nice new shoes, than putting my money towards feeding a poor person... or relaxing in a bubble bath rather than helping a friend pack boxes... or taking the best-looking piece of chocolate cake rather than leaving it for someone else... But most (or all!) of God's advice seems to work... and I've found this does, too.

> God promises that we will find joy when we lay down our lives and serve others.

When life as a parent gets tough, and you just want to bail, do it for Him, if you can't do it for your spouse or your kids right now. He will strengthen you with joy as you serve.

It Starts With You

When our responsibilities require us to fly, and we don't have the strength or the skill to crawl, we need to look outside of ourselves. "Those who hope in the Lord will renew their strength. They will soar on wings like eagles; they will run and not grow weary; they will walk and not be faint." (Isaiah 40:31)

God is the source. He has all wisdom, authority and power. I could never and would never bring up my children without Him.

When we are studying God's word we will find it incredible how it applies to the daily challenges we face in life. The bible assures us that it has value "for giving prudence to the simple, knowledge and discretion to the young." (Proverbs 1:4) Not only will it teach you how to teach your children, but it will also benefit you personally. "Let the wise listen and add to their learning, and let the discerning get guidance." (Proverbs 1:5)

God promises us that if we really seek Him and His ways, He will answer.

> Proverbs 2:1-6
> *If you accept my words and store up my commands within you, turning your ear to wisdom and applying your heart to understanding,*
> *and if you call out for insight and cry aloud for understanding,*
> *and if you look for it as for silver and search for it as for hidden treasure,*
> *then you will understand the fear of the Lord and find the knowledge of God.*
> *For the Lord gives wisdom, and from His mouth come knowledge and understanding.*

Everywhere I look, the bible is full of helpful guidelines for how to parent and just how to be, so that my kids can imitate me. God needs to be given the chance to mold your character so that you can be a good example to your kids. It starts with you. You need to let God do His work in you so that you are not hypercritical when expecting Godly character from your children. My children love it when I spend time with God, because they know that he changes me for the better. We don't have to be perfect, but we do need to show evidence that He is at work in us.

Being well-read, and memorising parts of the bible also has the advantage that when you are faced with a situation and ask Him for wisdom, you have a whole database of verses in your mind that He can call upon to give you guidance for that situation.

Caring for Yourself

Parenthood, and life, is an act of service, and our lives are so much more purposeful than just being about pleasing ourselves. However, a phrase that runs through my head frequently is one they say in the safety talk on the aeroplane: "Please apply your own mask first, before assisting children or fellow passengers."

It is just wisdom and common sense that we will be able to run a lot further and a lot faster when we are taking care of ourselves. When my children are all asking for something at once, and I am desperate for a wee, I take care of myself first, and then am able to concentrate on attending to their needs. If I am feeling lightheaded, I will feed myself first, and then be a loving, caring mom and be able to feed my children.

Get enough sleep, get enough exercise, get enough me-time, get enough food and water, and go to the loo! It is not selfish, it is essential, and your family will benefit for your wisdom.

Don't forget to have a little fun, and smile, smile, smile. You as parents can determine the mood in your home, and even mold your children's dispositions, by having a constant smile on your face, and laughter always ready.

Job Satisfaction

I think it's wonderful being a mom! I am never below my required quota of loves and kisses for the day!

Not too long ago, we found out we are expecting our fourth boy. Wow. What a thing. It is unimaginable to me that I would be so privileged to have four boys, and to still have the satisfaction and joy of bringing up two girls. It was never in my wildest dreams or plans for my life that I would be a mom to six, but then again, I had no idea of the sense of fulfilment I would get in bringing up my own children. I have such an incredible sense of job satisfaction in shaping and loving these children, it has exceeded any expectation I had of being a parent.

Don't get me wrong, I am pushed to the end of myself sometimes. It often seems like the hardest job in the world, certainly the hardest that I have experienced. But I'll never forget a lesson I learned in High School. In Grade 11 we had the job of decorating the school hall and organising the Matric dance, and, being a smaller school, we also attended the dance with the Matrics. We worked hard, day and night, to get it done, and I remember every detail of it. I remember the menu, I remember the gifts we gave the Matrics, I remember the decoration of each corner of the hall, even the men's loo's! But when we were in Matric, we got to just rock up at the dance, and someone else had done all the work. I hardly remember the theme of our Matric dance, let alone all the details. That always reminds me that the work that goes into something is most often directly proportional to the satisfaction and enjoyment you get out of it.

That is one of the reasons I am so determined to do as much of the 'childcare' hard work myself as possible. I try not to delegate bath time or spoon feeding or even nappy changing if I am able to do it myself. However, I have also learned to allow my husband the same privilege. With our first baby I would try to protect him from the hard work, knowing he had another full time job to attend to as well. But as our family has increased and I have relied on him more heavily with each baby and each pregnancy, he has loved being a dad more and more! (And he's an outstandingly brilliant and capable one - who knew?!) I had actually been denying him one of the greatest joys of his life in my effort to be helpful.

He sees

When the newborn is hungry, the toddler is sick, the preschooler is potty training at night, the six-year-old is teething her big teeth, and the eight-year-old is having nightmares, I can assure you that the most encouraging husband in the world can just not commend your toil enough! To describe all the non-stop demands you are seeing to to your husband, or a friend, just seems like moaning. When your hard work exceeds the amount of praise you are receiving for it, it is good to remember God's words to the church of Ephesus: Revelation 2:2 "I know your deeds, your hard work and perseverance." Isn't that great news? God knows. He was also awake all night, and He saw EVERYTHING. That is wonderful news that He sees all our deeds and hard work. It is also good to note that He carries on to say to the church in verse 4, "Yet I hold this against you: You have forgotten your first love." Having a God who sees everything, means He also sees the condition of our heart. So take courage that He sees your deeds, your hard work and your perseverance, and remember to keep loving Him as top of your agenda.

When I was writing the first chapters of this book, about the purpose of parenting, I was in my first trimester of pregnancy, incessantly nauseas, with a nine-month-old, a two-year-old, a four-year-old and two schoolgirls to run around, and it was really helpful to have to think about what the purpose of this all was. You know when you just can't take it anymore, and if it was possible to stop the world and get off, you would? But unlike deep-sea fishing, you can't turn the boat around and escape from it, and the nausea just won't end, so you need to find a reason to keep going. God wonderfully reminded me of the great and noble purposes of parenting – worth giving our lives for.

Now as I am ending off this book, I am heavily pregnant, immobile with displaced hips due to my fall, and constantly in pain and discomfort. I have had moments of frustration that leave me trying desperately to keep my tolerance levels, and I find myself needing to take a whole lot of my own advice. God is so kind and wise in that He has me constantly reminded by the writing of this book of the high standards required to imitate Him.

The wonderful thing about God, is that He knows that we are 'dust', and He loves us anyway. We don't serve our children, or our husbands, or our God, in order to earn anything. We do it because we have been given everything, and we want to serve God and show others how wonderful He is. Grace is a wonderful thing, and when we are not beating ourselves up about being below standard as parents, then we are guilt free, which makes it a whole lot easier to quickly apologise when we fall short, and keep moving forward.

When you live in a state of awareness of grace, your eyes are lifted up off of yourself, and you become aware of the beauty around you, and the wonders and joys of life. As my gaze is lifted by Him again, I feel ready to burst in excitement at the delicious joy of cradling one more newborn baby in the next few weeks! It is overwhelming and fabulous and intoxicating, and possibly the greatest joy this side of heaven.

I hope reading this has succeeded in giving you a few extra tools in your tool belt to help you do the best you can, but rest assured that God is working with you and He is not counting on you being perfect – but He was happy to give YOU the job of parenting your particular children anyway!

ABOUT THE AUTHOR

Jaci Mun-Gavin is the wife of a Christian pastor, Richard, and is the mother of two girls and four boys. Richard, Jaci, Jada Grace, Kiara, Jed, Rourke, Kade and Tyden make their home in Ramsgate, South Africa. Although qualified at the University of Cape Town as a robotics engineer, Jaci has a passion both for writing, and for loving, teaching and training her six children.